RAILWAY
WORLD
ANNUAL

RAILWAY WORLD

Annual 1975

Edited by
Alan Williams

LONDON

IAN ALLAN LTD

First published 1974

ISBN 0 7110 0547 8

© Ian Allan Ltd, 1974

Published by Ian Allan Ltd, Shepperton, Surrey,
and printed in the United Kingdom by
A. Wheaton & Co. Exeter.

Contents

6 A good year
7 Off to work on the Prison Line *V. Thompson*
12 London Transport trains *Photo feature*
18 Rails no more in Kirkcudbright *Photo feature*
26 The changing railways of Cornwall *Chris Heaps*
36 The 'Long Meg' *Derek Cross*
46 West of Swansea *Photo feature*
54 New light on the Salisbury disaster *J. T. Howard Turner*
65 Lincolnshire lines *Photo feature*
72 Diesels defunct *David Percival*
80 Southern in the Snow *Photo feature*
86 Metamorphosis on the other GCR *E. J. Alyson*
90 Towards the Tunnel? *Michael Rigby*
96 Battling towards Blaenau *Photo feature*
104 The lonely line *Derek Cross*
118 Last train on the 'Riverside' *Alan Young*
124 Pacifics Preserved *Photo feature*
128 The Barnstaple and Ilfracombe Railway *N. J. Brodrick*
134 'Madame' *Charles Long*

Front cover: Stanier class 5 4-6-0s Nos. 44874 and 45017 storm past Copy Pit with an SLS special on August 4 1968./*Derek Cross*

Title page: With Pennine snows on the ground, Stanier 8F 2-8-0 No. 48744 sets out from Buxton yard with a train of mineral empties in February 1968./*J. Patience*

A Good Year

It's going to be a good year for railway historians. Apart from marking the 150th anniversary of railways in Britain, it also looks very much as if it will mark the turning point in the future of railways – some have even suggested that a mini-Railway Mania is on the way. Personally, I doubt whether the resurgence will be quite as dynamic as that – although there can be no doubt that the now all-too-familiar twin energy and environmental crises have swung public opinion very much more in favour of railways.

This year, rather than attempt to compete with the myriad potted histories of railways that will undoubtedly appear on the bookstalls over the next few months, I have again attempted to put together more of a commentary which at once looks to the past, the present and the future. Perhaps the greatest potential event on the future railway horizon is the opening of the Channel Tunnel, which could be in being by 1980. Proposals for a tunnel link with France go back even before the railway era – the first, in fact, back to the time of the Anglo-French War. And it is almost a century since Sir Edward Watkin actively proposed a tunnel as the *pièce de résistance* of his grand scheme for a through Manchester–Paris trunk rail route. But as Michael Rigby shows in his piece 'Towards the Tunnel?', the very rivalry that served to kindle so many railway schemes in the 19th Century actually prevented Watkin's dream from becoming a reality, and it is only now, with unified, National rail networks on both sides of the Channel, that the project is approaching fruition.

For the present, Derek Cross takes a ride in the cab of a diesel on the West Highland line, and finds that the journey up to and across Rannoch Moor is every bit as awe inspiring as in steam days. And by way of contrast, he goes back in history just far enough to find steam engines still in action – to early summer 1967 – and tells the tale of what happens when four enthusiasts are let loose on a 9F climbing up to Ais Gill with 'the Long Meg.'

Going back into history, Victor Thompson describes the club-like atmosphere of commuting down from the top of Dartmoor on the now long-closed Princetown branch – the 'Prison Line' – while back even further, to the early hours of July 1, 1903, goes J. T. Howard Turner to seek out fresh evidence on the never-explained Salisbury disaster. These, plus Charles Long's strange encounter with 'Madame' and David Percival's 'Diesels Defunct', laced with several steam photo-features, seem a fair cross-section of the Railway World after 150 years.

Alan Williams

Off to Work on The Prison Line

V. THOMPSON

Lady Modiford's School nestled below the south-west rim of Dartmoor a mile from the line up at Dousland. From there, home was a five-mile walk with a bike up to Princetown, or twice that meandering distance by rail, five times a week. The winter of 1946 was a time when schoolmasters, if anybody, could afford the leisurely way.

Not that it was the best of times to take out that first season ticket. The approach to the station at Princetown was a long, barren path with nothing but fences to act as windbreaks and with no other use than to pen the ponies at the annual round-up. One morning at 7 am, I slogged through driving snow—backwards to keep my nipped lungs in operation —to arrive on the single platform only to discover that there was not a single rail in sight. Across the yard, snow made the engine shed windows look blankly yellow, not at all like the glaring orange warmth soon to be shared with the fireman who should have flashed his boiler an hour ago. The point was jabbed home by the gale, screaming down from Hessary Tor to propel you, willingly or not, into the Waiting Room. Only two of the familiar dozen or so regulars hunched beneath the gas jets. The young ones, pupils at the Grammar School at Tavistock, were either too tender or too experienced to turn out on a morning like this and dreamed of their masters, down in the fringe country, who would mark their registers with little black rings, glance at the ground frost outside and sigh about kids getting softer every year. A mass of crisp oilskins with a storm lantern bumbled through the door.

There would be no trains today. Someone had been on the 'phone from Dousland, the only other manned halt from here to Yelverton, to give warning of a three-foot wall of snow at the level crossing—which meant that you could expect something twice as high up at King Tor or Ingra. So there we all were with an unplanned holiday—provided we could survive the slog back home! No one seemed anxious to start.

There were reminiscences about the really bad fall (!) last year when it blew up late in the day to cut off the connection at Yelverton for the Princetown crowd returning from Plymouth and Tavistock. A bus was hurriedly chartered, but got only a mile or so to the arctic slopes of Peek Hill, still 1 in 5, before it took fright and returned its load to Yelverton so that the passengers could spend a memorable night in slimly staffed hotels at the Company's expense.

But with the thaw came all the privileges of commuting on the prison line. The 7.30 am was not so much a train as a travelling club of regulars with occasional guest-members out for a day's shopping in Plymouth. Clerks, pupils and warders' wives fitted into one coach, with corner seats for most of us. There was a second coach, taken out for an airing on special days, such as Tavistock Goosey Fair; or in August for the holiday crowds which descended (ascended?) on Princetown in torrents of (10?) on Bank Holidays; and for the Saturday night train every week of the year.

Two crews served the 2-6-2T. Driver Gough shared a passion for darts with the Dartmoor run which came as a surprise when you heard his Cockney accent. Never a regret for old Smoky—that weathered face was part of the route, as rugged as the tors. On the 7.30 am down he would leave his fireman in charge of the cab and make a rough check of the roll, for he had the reputation of never losing a passenger. He would stand alongside the coach, blanketed in steam, and give gentle encouragement to a last-minute sprinter down the station drive. To my knowledge, time and Bill's patience ran out

Above: **In typical Dartmoor winter weather, 4500 class 2-6-2T No. 4568 rolls away from Ingra Tor Halt with the 12.08 Princetown–Yelverton train in February 1956, just a fortnight before the closure of the branch.**/*P. F. Bowles*

only once—I arrived just in time to see the tail lamp of the early morning train disappearing past the box. But the watchful signalman waggled the 'distant' in their own private code for 'Did you leave something?'— and back came the 7.30 am for the lost sheep to be gathered in! But then, the Great Western always claimed the record for personal service.

Now and again strangers would stand aloof from the 7.30 club to commandeer the first compartment for a solitary traveller. Beneath those civvy clothes you could recognise the escort as one of the warders. His charge could be an arsonist, a larcenist or a con-man. But whatever, he was now an ex-con. Shepherding the time-served man away was not so much a courtesy as an assurance that he was safely off the premises, away from contacts inside! One morning, all protocol defied, I shared the man's compartment and he told me his life story long before reaching the halt at King Tor. He had run a radio shop in Cardiff until chain stores and the wholesalers brought in the bailiffs. It was a choice between his family's foundations or a fire in the basement. Back in the bar that evening I railed about justice and a five-year sentence until the steward declared it to be a human interest story never put on his files—meaning the prison records which were his charge, and also that he would not have been led all the way up the path to King Tor, short as it was!

King Tor was the first halt on the road from Princetown, a gaunt, wooden deck as barren as the moor, standing on high stilts like something with its trousers rolled up in waves of heather. Through summery haze you might glimpse the quarries at Merrivale but it was a desolate spot more suited to winter fog and Conan-Doyle's Hound of the Baskervilles. There was menace, too, in the old iron sign warning travellers, under the protective runes of 'G.W.R.', to keep their dogs on a leash for fear of snakes. Nobody ever turned up to benefit, with or without dog, but there was once a night of rain when a coach door thumped and the guard returned a cheery 'Goodnight' to someone out there in the dark.

From here the line looped around in descent to Ingra Tor, with its tiny siding petering out among the rocks, and you could listen a minute or two for an early lark lost in the glare of sunrise. Lambs in Spring would lose themselves in a mix of scattered granite, while in Summer the stones would resolve themselves into groups of somnolent sheep. Then we were off and away to the bridge at the foot of Peek Hill with Walkhampton church prodding darkly from a winter landscape to assure one that the moor was not such a God-forsaken place. Pine trees crowded the line quite suddenly here, shutting out the moorland brightness. But only for a moment, then you came down the bank high above the dam at Burrator, where someone in his wisdom had built another long-legged halt to take it all in. It could not have been built for the water-board men— they were heard but never seen, except for an empty trestle hanging over the bridge or a giant's cotton-reel of cable lying nearby. In fact, of course, everybody knew they lived deep down at the foot of The Wall in a pygmy-sized hut where they spent the day making waterfall sounds! In April, that is, when the rains kept a spindrift of foam lining the high side of the dam.

By late summer, you would be reminded of the Burrator legend of a drowned village and a church spire which pierced the lake in times of drought. Fantasy would dwindle all through September with the receding water line and only Sheepstor, rugged and high on the far bank, ever pierced the water, upside-down in mirrored symmetry. A narrow road always empty, arrowed across the bridge, and then swung immediately to the left to avoid a wood and parted from the lakeside to pass the hamlet where three white Rajah Brooks, tired of the tropics, now preferred the peace of a moorland churchyard.

Once through the crossing gates at Dousland, the moor seemed miles away. Even in January, stepping out onto the platform brought a sudden mildness and hawthorn hedges sheltered every step of the mile to the coke-stove and smoke of the village classroom. After the end of school at four, the climb back demanded an hour to think about it as you soaked up the pot-bellied warmth all to yourself, but one evening I sat out the time in the Waiting Room at Dousland instead.

Driver Gough broke a rule and kept a pledge to take me on the footplate that summer evening. I was propped well back

Below: **Churchward's 4400 class 2-6-2Ts also found employment on the 'Prison Line'. Here No. 4410 restarts its single-coach train from Dousland in brilliant sunshine on July 5, 1955.**/*R. C. Riley*

against the coal bunker for my own safety and just in case one of the management should be wandering around south of Bristol. The problem was hearing rather than seeing; Bill and his fireman chatted in signs and I never realised the age-old silence of the moors could be so shattered or heal so quickly. A scream from the whistle was soaked up by the furze on Sharpitor and the old red fox at which it was aimed was just as undisturbed. It was mangy and old enough to have watched the first tramway run by, downhill with granite and back up with fertiliser for the prison settlement. It was sunning itself on a vast stone li-lo and tilted its head in bare acknowledgement of the loco's need to

Below: **Further up the climb towards Princetown, at King Tor Halt, we find 4410 again, toiling around the slopes on the last stages of its climb across Dartmoor.**

Bottom: **The Princetown branch did not exactly serve a densely-populated part of the land—as this shot of 4410 running into Ingra Tor Halt in July 1955 clearly shows! Indeed, in such a desolate location, one wonders just who the halts were meant to serve.**/*R. C. Riley*

let off steam about the daily grind to Ingra. Up to King Tor, the fireman had enough to do to beat the steady climb but as we coasted down to Princetown he interrupted his airing to slam shut the regulator. We came to a protesting stop by the hut circles above Devil's Elbow. Surely nothing but the line up or an attempted suicide could cause a crisis here? The crew jumped down to the gravel, leaving me in sole charge of the cab, and I watched a two-minute tussle with a ram which had tangled its horns with the wire fence. All this was part and parcel of the Dartmoor haul—timetables gave way happily to man or beast along its narrow but not-so-straight path.

Sunday for the railway was a day of rest— all very proper after the Saturday high-spot of the week. Saturday was also Christmas, Easter, VE Day—the day of the two-coach run. There was only one snag. Saturday out ended on the platform at Millbay, Plymouth at 6 pm and was really a Saturday 'in'—In familiar company, In the warm, In a train.

That first lap up to Yelverton could flop if you shared a compartment with foreigners from Shaugh Vale or Tavvy. With no common language you stared from a corner seat at the shunting yards at Laira, where the Southern line branched off to the right to its own terminus at Friary. You could always bet there would be an up train out of Friary waiting for the road here, giving proper deference to the Western's right of way or perhaps just waiting to watch the prison crowd go by. Then the Plym, pouring down from the clay-pits milk-white. A short stop at Marsh Mills and we would tunnel into Plym Woods and skirt the old clay-line to Plymbridge. Once as a child I had spent a night on the lamp-lit platform here, holding on to a faint hope that there might be another train home, late as it was, and gripping a straw basket filled with nothing but blackberry stains. Maybe it was a punishment for adventures earlier in the day when we sat on the wooden summit of the clay-wagon ramp with an unhooked tub and devised Arnold Ridley plots to kill the 2.30 to Tavvy. As

children that line up to Shaugh had been our alma-mater, had taught us where to find tadpoles and trout, the seasons for strawberries, primrose and sloes, and how to use dock leaves for stings. After that one overnight stay at Plymbridge, it taught us how to read little way-side time-tables, too!

Down towards Shaugh the loco would send a whistle bouncing on ahead—there's no echo like that in a wooded valley. We would pass high above a flooded clay-pit blue with mystery, then forget it as we came out into the brightness of the Meavy. Yelverton was half-way house, re-union time. Nothing could subdue the excitement, not even gas jets in November fog. Friends and families, clans of the hill-top tribes, coalesced into little groups as they moved up and over the footbridge to the platform where the connection simmered. Back in the Tavistock train, the lowlanders shifted seats and compartments and watched the Saturday night fair in dour silence, wondering no doubt how outcasts could share such high spirits. They went off to Horrabridge or a late tea in Tavvy with no more thoughts of us heading out into the darkness, the tors and a wind gibbering in the wires. We left all that to Bill and his mate while back in the warmth the talk was of bargains at Dingles, or the film at the Gaumont.

There were the usual protests and petitions when they said the line must close, but inevitably the State and the bus won the battle. You wonder whether Princetown folk feel any loss these days, for the prison staff is subject to frequent transfers and retirements, and the moor has little to offer the young leaving school. It's commoner now to see a car at the kerb, but four people in a Ford do not make a club.

The rails came up soon after closure, leaving a highway for the sheep and the foxes, all of which are as indifferent to it as that old red fellow we woke at Sharpitor. Budgets and losses do little to balance all the original planning and the toil with all that now remains, a narrow gravel scar across the face of the moor.

London Transport Trains

Below: At first glance, London Transport's railways can appear very uniform and uninteresting. But on closer examination, as these next few pages show, there is a surprising variety, both in types of rolling stock and areas served. In fact, London's Underground proves still to be every bit as cosmopolitan as the capital it serves. For instance, much of the system, once away from the heart of the city, runs above ground; here, on one such section, a Metropolitan Line train bound for Watford nears journeys end as it curves through the tree-lined cutting at Croxley in July 1967./*P. H. Groom*

Above Right: **Paradoxically for an all-electric railway, London Transport's small stud of steam engines outlived their sisters on BR metals by several years. Indeed, the last LT steam engines in traffic were in fact ex-GW Pannier tanks purchased from BR; here, 0-6-0PT No. L95 rumbles through Harrow-on-the-Hill on August 18, 1969 bound for Neasden Depot with empty rubbish wagons from Croxley tip.**/*G. S. Cocks*

Below right: **This Piccadilly Line train running into Hounslow West station in the Summer of 1971 is typical of everyday life on LT. But even this will soon be a period piece, for work is now well advanced on the Piccadilly Line extension to Hatton Cross and London (Heathrow) Airport, and once it is complete, Hounslow West will cease to be the western terminus of the line.**/*P. R. Foster*

Left: **You might think that a tube train looks a little incongruous on a single-line branch in rural Essex, but this is Ongar, northern extremity of the Central Line, with the 15.38 shuttle to Epping waiting to depart on May 1, 1971.**/*J. Rickard*

Right: **Amidst a collection of engineer's battery-electric locomotives, ex-GW 5700 class 0-6-0PT No. L95 sends a plume of steam skywards as it bustles about the yard at Lillie Bridge Depot, near Olympia, in February 1970.**/*J. H. Cooper-Smith*

Below: **The Underground goes over the water—a four car Metropolitan Line train from Baker Street to Watford clatters across the viaduct spanning the Grand Union Canal at Cassiobury in February 1970.**/*C. T. Gifford*

Left: **The only electric trains ever to penetrate the bastions of Paddington were those of the Metropolitan Railway. Here, one of their successors pauses at the WR terminus on a Whitechapel–Hammersmith working in June 1971.**/*Michael Baker*

Below: **A surprise for passengers at Harrow-on-the-Hill on this bright July day in 1972—veteran Metropolitan Railway electric locomotive No. 5** *John Hampden* **pauses before departing for Uxbridge with an enthusiasts brake van special.**/*G. D. King*

These views of Bakerloo and Metropolitan Line trains at Wembley Park in July, 1970, serve to illustrate the difference in size between 'tube' and 'surface' stock. The Bakerloo Line train (*Above right***) is formed of 1938 tube stock in the now obsolescent traditional red livery, while the Metropolitan Line Watford train (***below right***) is formed of A60 stock in the now-standard unpainted aluminium finish. The Stanmore branch of the Bakerloo Line will become the northern part of the new Fleet Line when the in-town tube sections, now under construction, are complete.**/*D. N. Bradley (2)*

Rails No More
in Kirkcudbright

Below: **One of the cross-country routes which succumbed completely to the Beeching Axe in the 1960's was the ex-Glasgow & South Western and Portpatrick & Wigtownshire Joint line from Dumfries west through Kirkcudbright to Stranraer. Trains still serve Stranraer along the coast from the north, and now the boat trains have to use this more circuitous route via Ayr to reach their destination.**
Gatehouse of Fleet was the summit of the P&WJ, and it is here, in Summer 1963, before the axe fell that we find Stanier Class 5 4-6-0 No. 44723 hurrying west with a Dumfries–Stranraer local./*Derek Cross*

Above right: **Both running tender-first, BR Standard Class 6 4-6-2 No. 72009** *Clan Stewart* **pilots Stanier Class 5 4-6-0 No. 44925 around the curve into Dumfries with the empty stock of a special to Castle Douglas in May 1964.**/*Derek Cross*

Below right: **P&WJ trains had their own bay platforms at Dumfries; here Fairburn Class 4 2-6-4Ts Nos 42689 and 42196 make a vigorous start alongside the G&SWR main line on July 26, 1963 with a local train which will divide at Castle Douglas for Stranraer and Kirkcudbright.**/*Derek Cross*

Left: **Late spring 1968 saw demolition work on the P&WJ in full swing; one track has already gone as BR/Sulzer Bo-Bo No. D7620 growls across the picturesque Goldilea Viaduct with a train of reclaimed rail and sleepers.**/*Derek Cross*

Above right: **The countryside grew more rugged as the line struck west to its summit at Gatehouse of Fleet, but BR Standard Class 6 Pacific No. 72006** *Clan MacKenzie* **was coping well with its ten-coach troop special for Stranraer as it neared the summit one day in June 1965.**/*Derek Cross*

Below right: **BR Standard Class 4 Mogul No. 76073 rolls gently off the Kirkcudbright branch at Castle Douglas and prepares to swing across to the up line with a train for Dumfries on June 11, 1963.**/*Derek Cross*

Below: **With the waters of Loch Ken as a backdrop, BR Standard 2-6-4T No. 80061 hurries away from the tiny station at Parton with a Dumfries–Stranraer local on June 7, 1965.**/*Derek Cross*

Left : **Garlieston was at the end of a short branch from Millisle, itself on the Whithorn branch from Newton Stewart. And nature had already begun to reclaim the little-used tracks here when, in May 1964, BR Standard Class 2 2-6-0 No. 78016 arrived to shunt the yard.**/*Derek Cross*

Below left : **A few months later, in September 1964, sister engine No. 78026 was on the same duty, seen here near Wigtown on the return trip to Newton Stewart.**/*Derek Cross*

Right : **Before its demise, the Whithorn branch saw its share of special trains including this RCTS/SLS Special seen at Red Moss, near Wigtown in June 1962 in the charge of Preserved Caledonian Single No. 123 and GNSR 4-4-0 No. 49** *Gordon Highlander.*/*Derek Cross*

Below : **Kirkcudbright was the terminus of the G&SWR line from Dumfries. On June 11, 1963, Fairburn Class 4 2-6-4T No. 42689 busies itself about a yard which could even then clearly still support a remunerative freight traffic.**/*Derek Cross*

Left: **Stanier Class 5 4-6-0 No. 45158** *Glasgow Yeomanry* **clatters past Newton Stewart West box with a party special bound for Dumfries on May 28, 1964.**/*Derek Cross*

Below: **Moguls together: it is September 1964 and BR Standard Class 4 2-6-0 No. 76072 waits to restart a train for Stranraer from Newton Stewart, while alongside, Class 2 2-6-0 No. 78016 stands patiently with the Whithorn branch goods.**/*Derek Cross*

Top right: **With its cylinder drains open, BR Standard 2-6-4T No. 80119 makes a dramatic exit from Newton Stewart with a two-coach local for Dumfries on September 18, 1964.**/*Derek Cross*

Middle right: **Caledonian 2F 0-6-0 No. 57375 blows off steam impatiently below the bridge at Newton Stewart as it waits to start off down the Whithorn branch with an SLS special in April 1963.**/*Derek Cross*

Bottom right: **Just five years later, in May 1968, the scene at Newton Stewart has changed very much for the worse; the last passengers have long since departed, and the once-neat platforms are now littered with the detritus of the demolition gangs. Soon the last sections of track will be lifted, and there will be rails no more in Kirkcudbright.**/*Derek Cross*

Hurrying past Wearde signal box, between St. Germans and Saltash, comes the 8.15 Perranporth–Paddington train on July 13, 1957, double-headed over this section by County Class 4-6-0 No. 1007 *County of Brecknock* and 4300 class 2-6-0 No. 5357./*R. E. Vincent*

The Changing Railways of Cornwall

CHRIS HEAPS

My earliest childhood railway memories are of a Great Western branch line terminus in Cornwall, to which I was regularly taken on sunny afternoons. I can recall how bells would sound in the signal box, how the home signal would be lowered and how promptly on time a green tank engine would hustle under the road bridge at the approach to the station hauling two GWR branch line coaches. Its arrival would be followed by a short burst of frenzied activity, with passengers alighting and parcels being unloaded, whereupon the locomotive would be detached from the two coaches and would run around the train. Peace would then be restored as the engine rejoined the train and then simmered in the sunlight until its next departure an hour or more later.

That scene is now part of history, and the station on which I spent so many happy hours has been razed to the ground and the site incorporated in a new road. During the last twelve years or so, the majority of the GWR's Cornish branch lines have been closed and all but a fraction of the ex-London and South Western Railway 'withered arm' in Cornwall has been abandoned. The Duchy lives in fear of the closure of the whole system from Plymouth, but it is to be hoped that social and environmental arguments will overcome any economic basis for proposals of such magnitude.

Although the Duchy of Cornwall is now linked in the public eye with holiday makers and the tourist trade, in the 19th century it was one of the more industrialised areas

of Britain, its economy depending upon the tin and copper mines that flourished throughout the county and particularly in the Camborne-Redruth area in the west. One of the early railway inventors, Richard Trevithick, was born near Camborne and as early as 1809 the construction of the first tramway in the county had commenced from the mining district of Poldice near Scorrier (near Redruth) to the north coast port of Portreath. This line, not 'a public railway' in the legal sense of the term, was disused by the mid 1860s. Other early mineral railways, built to the narrow gauges of 4 ft and 2 ft 6 in, were built respectively between the Redruth district and Devoran (on a tributary of the River Fal on the south coast) and between St Austell and Pentewan during the 1820s. Both the Redruth and Chasewater Railway and the Pentewan Railway were originally worked by horse power and did not officially carry passengers, and both expired during or soon after the First World War when the mines that they had been built to serve ceased production. The Pentewan Railway was unusual in that it was originally constructed without Parliamentary consent, its existence not being officially recognised until 40 years later by the incorporation of the Pentewan Railway and Harbour Company Limited in 1873.

Although to one born in west Cornwall the term 'railway' is synonymous with the Great Western Railway, it must not be forgotten that the London and South Western Railway (later the Southern Railway) operated the oldest standard gauge railway in the county and one of the oldest in the country—the Bodmin and Wadebridge Railway. This line was opened in 1834 and was operated by locomotives from the outset. Part of the line is still in use for goods traffic. It is remembered not only as the last outpost of the Beattie 2-4-0 WTs, which remained in use on the Wenford Bridge branch of the Bodmin and Wadebridge railway until 1962, when they were almost 90 years old, but also because it gave the LSWR its first foothold in the county. The LSWR purchased the Bodmin

The independent Liskeard and Looe Railway existed as an entirely separate, isolated system for over 20 years, its northerly terminus being situated at Moorswater, beneath the Cornwall Railway's viaduct west of Liskeard. But in 1901, a steep and sharply curved spur was built from Coombe Junction —seen (*left*) in August 1954 with GW 4500 Class 2-6-2T No. 5502 departing for Looe—up to the main line at Liskeard. And it is at Liskeard (Change for Looe!) on June 24, 1955 that we find BR Standard Class 4 4-6-0 No. 75028 (*below*) sauntering through on the up line with a class H freight./*R. C. Riley: R. E. Vincent*

and Wadebridge Railway in 1846, at a time when its nearest outpost was still more than 200 miles away. This acquisition had not been sanctioned by Parliament and was not formally approved until 40 years later by the London and South Western Railway Act of 1886. The line remained isolated from the rest of the LSWR system until the opening of the final section of the North Cornwall line between Halwill and Wadebridge in 1895, although it was connected to the national system some seven years earlier with the opening in 1888 of the link with the GWR Bodmin Road-Bodmin General branch constructed in the previous year. History has now been reversed, and although the Wenford Bridge section of the original line is still in use for goods, all traffic is now taken once again over the link to Bodmin Road and the GWR, the LSWR North Cornwall system having been closed and all track lifted.

Bodmin Road was opened in 1859, when the main section of the GWR main line was opened by the Cornwall Railway between Saltash on the Cornish boundary and Truro. To the west of Truro, the West Cornwall Railway had already opened in 1852, having previously taken over the assets of the Hayle Railway which had operated a narrow gauge and partly incline-worked system from 1837 between Hayle and Gwennap (a mining village in the Camborne/Redruth district). Part of the old route was incorporated in the West Cornwall line, the rope incline sections being abandoned when the new line was completed. The West Cornwall Railway was constructed to the standard gauge of 4 ft 8½ in, whereas the Cornwall Railway was built to Brunel's GWR 7 ft 0½ in broad gauge. The West Cornwall Railway was required by parliamentary powers to lay additional broad gauge tracks between Truro and Penzance in 1866 and through broad gauge trains commenced running between Paddington and Penzance for the first time in the following year. The standard gauge tracks were retained in use, however, and goods trains made up of both standard and broad

gauge wagons formed an unusual operating feature of the line between 1871 and 1892.

Although the West Cornwall Railway was transferred to the GWR, the Bristol and Exeter Railway and the South Devon Railway from January 1, 1866, and became the absolute property of the GWR on August 1, 1878, the company was not wound up as provided for by the West Cornwall Railway Act of 1865. The company therefore continued in nominal existence, notwithstanding the 1923 Grouping, until transferred to the British Transport Commission by the Transport Act of 1947.

Many of the branch lines joining the main line were built as broad gauge railways, including that between Truro and Falmouth, opened by the Cornwall Railway in 1863, and between St Erth and St Ives, the last to be built to the broad gauge, opened by the GWR in 1877. Even while it was under construction, it was already obvious that the standard gauge would eventually reign supreme, and the Cornish system was finally converted in 1892 during the weekend of May 20/21. The massive job of converting 177 miles of track was completed during the weekend as planned. On Friday, May 20, the 'Cornishman' left Paddington at 10.15 am hauled by the broad gauge locomotive *Great Britain* and arrived at Penzance a little late at 9 pm, having been delayed by ceremonies at stations along the line. On Monday, May 23, the up 'Cornishman' left Penzance for London at 11.10 am, formed of standard gauge stock and the broad gauge was dead.

The conversion of the main line to standard gauge did not mark, however, the final major reconstruction of the line. The Great Western main line in Cornwall is famous for the multiplicity of viaducts, embankments and cuttings necessitated by the topography of the county. Between Saltash and Penzance there were originally no less than 40 viaducts, the longest (Truro) of 443 yards and the highest (St Pinnock) of 151 feet, closely followed by Liskeard of 150 feet and Moorswater of 147 feet. Five of these viaducts were demolished when the new diversionary line to the west of Saltash was opened in 1908. All were originally of all-wooden Brunel construction built (with the exception of the five viaducts abandoned in 1908) on masonry piers, each of which had to be replaced between 1871 and 1934 by granite and metal structures. The last Brunel timber viaduct to remain in use on a passenger carrying railway—College Wood Viaduct at Penryn on the Falmouth branch—was not replaced until 1934. The reconstruction of these viaducts was necessitated not only because of the original slender and temporary nature of the structures, but also because the main line was doubled between Saltash and Penzance in sections after 1893. The bulk of the line had been doubled by the beginning of the First World War, although the final sections between St Erth and Marazion, and between Scorrier and Drump Lane (near Redruth) were not completed until 1929 and 1930 respectively. From April 13, 1930, the whole of the Cornwall Railway and West Cornwall Railway main line from Plymouth to Penzance had been doubled, with the sole exception of the section over the Royal Albert Bridge Saltash—the railway gateway to Cornwall—designed by Brunel and opened by Prince Albert in 1859. In recent years, a small section of line over and adjoining Largin viaduct near Liskeard has been reduced again to single track to avoid expensive repairs which would otherwise be required, and it may be anticipated that further sections will be so treated when the whole county comes within the proposed control of the power signal box at Plymouth North Road.

In addition to the branch lines to Bodmin, St Ives and Falmouth already mentioned, other branches were opened as feeders to the main Cornwall Railway and West Cornwall Railway main line. Lines were open to passengers between Fowey and Par and Newquay in 1876, between Lostwithiel and Fowey in 1895, between Moorswater (near Liskeard) and Looe by the independent Liskeard and Looe Railway in 1879 and between Helston and Gwinear Road by the Helston Railway in 1887. The Moorswater-Looe line, which originally terminated almost 150 feet below the Cornwall Railway viaduct, was extended by a steep and sharply curved link to join the main line in 1901 and the independent company was vested in the GWR by the Grouping in 1923. The last branch to be opened—between Newquay and Chacewater in 1905—was unusual in that the greater part of the line had been originally constructed for mineral purposes only, the passenger line being completed by the construction of the western half of the line between Chacewater and Shepherds to join up with a mineral railway (then brought up to passenger line standards) constructed 30 years earlier.

Traffic on the main line has always included a fair proportion of both goods and passenger traffic, the line in recent years having been graced not only by the world famous 'Cornish Riviera Limited' but also by the 'Cornishman' from Bradford and 'The Royal Duchy' from Paddington. After the grouping, all types of GWR locomotives were permitted on the main line, with the exception only of the King and 47XX classes, although BR Standard Britannia Class Pacifics (especially Nos. 70016/19/21/24) were used briefly in the mid-1950s. Hall and Grange class 4-6-0s were the most common locomotives in use in the county in the later years of steam and were suitable for both passenger and goods work, while Castles, Manors, Counties and 43XX moguls were used in lesser numbers. On the passenger branch trains the 4500 and 4575 2-6-2T tanks reigned supreme, the 0-6-0PTs being used mainly for shunting work and on the china clay lines in the Par area. St Blazey, the shed for the china clay lines, generally included two 2-8-0T locomotives of the 42XX class among its allocation, these being used on the Par-Fowey china clay trains, particularly on the line through the Pinnock tunnel that has recently been converted into a privately-owned roadway operated by English China Clays Limited.

Above: **It's time to get up, for Castle class 4-6-0 No. 5003** *Lulworth Castle* **is nearing journeys end as it restarts the previous night's 23.50 Paddington–Penzance sleepers away from Hayle.**/*J. C. Beckett*

Right: **Before the days of mechanised permanent way work, with its long-welded rails and concrete sleepers, GW 4500 class 2-6-2T No. 4565 simmers gently in the sun on a September Sunday in 1951 while the gang unload sleepers alongside the main line between Par and St. Austell.**/*P. M. Alexander*

Below: **Hall class 4-6-0 No. 6912** *Helmster Hall* **rattles across the junction to the St. Ives branch and into St. Erth station with a down stopping train in June 1952 while on the right another member of the class prepares to depart up the main line with a train of milk tanks.**/*B. A. Butt*

The Great Western main line in Cornwall was amongst the first in the county to be dieselised in the late 1950s and the early 1960s. The first main line locomotives to invade the county were Warship class diesels of the D6XX type, followed by the later (Class 42) Warship engines and the Class 52 Western diesel hydraulics. The Warships have already been withdrawn, and the Westerns are now being rapidly replaced by Class 45 and Class 47 diesel-electric locomotives displaced from other parts of Britain. On the branch lines, the North British Class 22 diesel-hydraulic locomotives that took over from the prairie and pannier tanks have also been withdrawn, and have been replaced on the remaining branches by Class 25 locomotives.

At the beginning of the 1960s Cornwall was unique amongst counties in not having suffered the loss of any passenger lines since the Second World War. The first blow fell in 1962, when passenger services were withdrawn on November 3 from the Helston-Gwinear Road branch. Any feeling by the inhabitants of Helston that they were being victimised was soon dispelled, however, by the closures within six months of the Plymouth-Launceston and the Chacewater-Newquay branches. Since then, the Lostwithiel-Fowey and Bodmin Road-Bodmin General/Wadebridge lines have also closed to passenger traffic.

Far more drastic—indeed fatal—has been the pruning of the ex-LSWR lines in North Cornwall, the 'withered arm' of the Southern Railway, which was dismembered within two years of its transfer to Western Region Management at the beginning of 1963. From Halwill Junction in Devon, lines were opened in 1898 to Bude (of which the last 4½ miles fall within Cornwall) and progressively between 1886 and 1899 to Launceston, Camelford, Wadebridge and Padstow. 'The Atlantic Coast Express' incorporated through coaches from Waterloo to both Bude and Padstow until its withdrawal in 1964. This express was hauled in later years by Bulleid West Country and Battle of Britain Pacifics,

although the mainstay of the locomotive stock on the North Cornwall lines was for many years provided by Maunsell Class N and U 2-6-0s, and the ever popular and long-lived Drummond T9 Class Greyhound 4-4-0s introduced in 1899. Reference has already been made to the three Beattie well-tanks (BR Nos 30585/6/7) which survived until December 1962 at Wadebridge for work on the Wenford Bridge branch. They were replaced for a short time by the ex-GWR pannier tanks of the 1366 class, but were soon replaced themselves by diesel shunters. On the North Cornwall line, diesel multiple-units were introduced by the Western Region after it took control, but passenger trains were withdrawn from the North Cornwall line in October 1966 and three months later on the line from Bodmin to Wadebridge and Padstow. Ironically, a new station had opened only two years earlier, in 1964, at Boscarne Junction, where the ex-Bodmin and Wadebridge line to Bodmin North and the link line leading to the Great Western at Bodmin General met. It was a small halt, named Boscarne Junction Exchange Platform. It enabled the Bodmin North branch to be re-organised as a feeder line to the Bodmin Road-Bodmin General-Wadebridge service and was operated until its closure by a four-wheel diesel railbus.

Further east, on the county boundary with Devon, another ex-Southern Railway branch has all but disappeared. The Bere Alston to Callington branch remains in truncated form between Bere Alston and Gunnislake only, retained because of the isolated location of Calstock on the west bank of the River Tamar, some miles from the nearest road bridges over the river. To the north, the river can be crossed near Tavistock, whilst downstream road crossings were limited to two chain ferries until the opening of the Saltash suspension bridge immediately along-side Brunel's structure in the early 1960s. Part of this line had originally been con-structed as a 3 ft 6 in narrow gauge industrial railway by the East Cornwall Mineral Railway; in 1891 it was taken over by the

Plymouth Devonport and South Western Junction Railway, which converted the line to standard gauge and constructed the connecting line across Calstock viaduct, 120 feet above the Tamar, to the LSWR main line at Bere Alston. The new line was opened throughout in 1908. The PDSWJR never formed part of the LSWR, passing directly into the ownership of the Southern Railway at the Grouping in 1923. The branch is now worked by two-car diesel multiple-units from Plymouth, reversing at Bere Alston, the ex-LSWR main line thence to Okehampton and Exeter around the northern edge of Dartmoor having been abandoned as far as Okehampton in 1967.

Of the railways mentioned, only the main line between Saltash Bridge and Penzance, and the grant-aided branches to St Ives, Falmouth, Newquay (from Par) and Looe remain. The track was removed from most of the closed lines soon after their demise and the trackbeds are rapidly reverting to nature, the cuttings filling with wild rhododendron bushes, the embankments becoming covered with gorse and many flat sections being re-incorporated in the adjoining fields. Most metal bridges have been demolished, but the granite structures seem likely to remain for years as evidence of the past. Many stations have already been demolished or vandalised, including the branch terminus at Helston which discerning readers will have recognised as that so imprinted upon my memory!

It is to be hoped that the county will be spared further closures. A decade later, experience of the effects of the closure of the Helston branch has shown just how many local inhabitants are seriously affected by the removal of a local communication link—especially when, as in the Helston case, the alternative bus service required as a condition of closure by the local Transport Users Consultative Committee is also subsequently withdrawn.

Such branch lines provided a friendly and reliable service that formed part of the fabric of local life—a factor which cannot be quantified and therefore was not taken into account by the short-sighted economists and planners of the road-orientated Ministry of Transport who recommended and carried out the closures. Now the current resurgence of interest in the railway system and the beginnings of a realisation of the follies of the Beeching era have come too late to save the lines already closed and abandoned. Cornwall must now hope that it will suffer no more attacks on the remains of its railway system.

There are well over 30 viaducts on the main line between Saltash and Penzance, and all were originally Brunel all-wood structures on masonry piers. But the increasing weight of trains, and the doubling of the line, meant that all eventually had to be replaced by granite and steel structures, of which St. Germans viaduct—seen here in July 1973 as a Class 52 diesel-hydraulic C-C crosses with a down express—is a fine example./*J. H. Cooper-Smith*

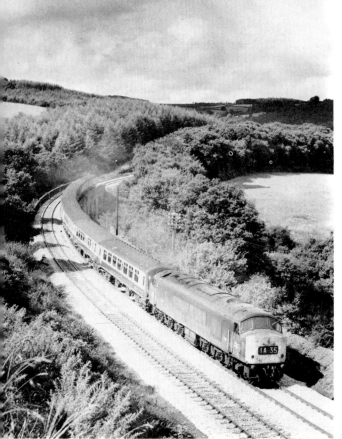

Nowadays, the diesel engine reigns supreme over the remaining lines in Cornwall; express passenger and freight trains are worked by diesel locomotives such as Class 45 1Co-Co1 No. 149 (*left*) at the head of the up "Cornish Riviera" in the lush countryside near Bodmin Road, while the remaining branch and stopping services are the province of the ubiquitous suburban railcar—this three-car set (*below*) pauses at the now "rationalised" St. Ives terminus before returning to St. Erth on September 2, 1970./*Michael Baker*

Right: **Perhaps the smallest station built by BR, Boscarne Junction Exchange Platform was constructed in 1964. It was built to enable the diesel railbus on the ex-LSWR line from Bodmin North to connect with the Bodmin Road–Wadebridge service at Boscarne Junction, and survived until all passenger services were withdrawn from both lines two years later.**/*Chris Heaps*

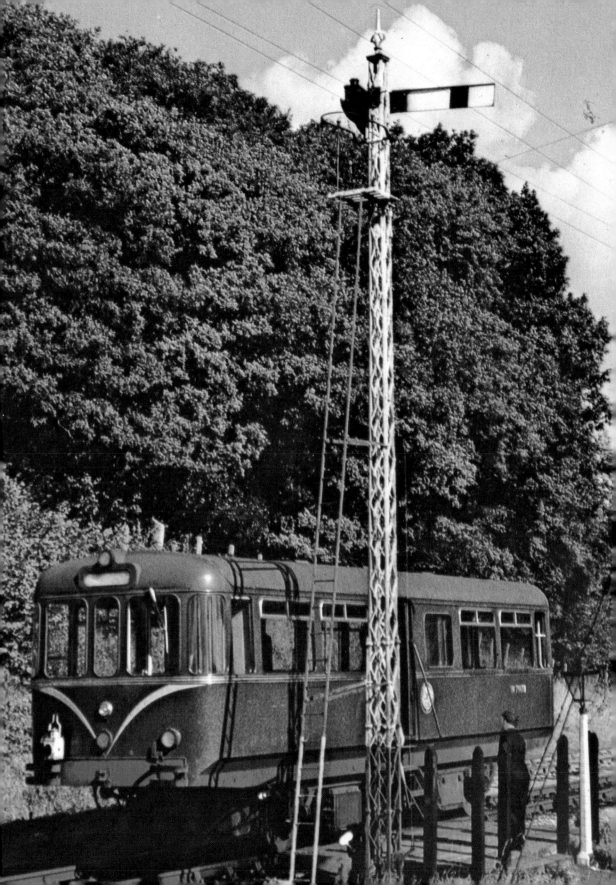

The 'Long Meg'

DEREK CROSS

"Who killed steam engines?
I, said the Accountant,
With my pen and ink-pot,
I killed steam engines!"

The great thing about nursery rhymes is that, under the jingles, there is often a very fundamental truth; they are also very easy to parody, sometimes with an even more fundamental truth. The sad saga of 'Cock Robin' comes to mind in writing about a trip in 1967 on a goods train over the High Pennines from Carlisle to Blea Moor for the name of the train, unofficially of course, was the afternoon 'Long Meg'—and there was something rather like a nursery rhyme about that.

There was, however, nothing remotely nursery-like about its working, for it was officially train 6F56, the 13.20 from the quarry at Long Meg Sidings on the banks of the Eden between Carlisle and Appleby, conveying anhydrite ore for the manufacture of sulphuric acid to the giant ICI plant at Widnes. In the penultimate year of steam it was probably the hardest regular steam working in the country. There were three such trains in the course of the day, but the afternoon turn had the reputation of being the hardest and also the most tightly timed. Through the courtesy of the LMR's Preston Division I had obtained a foot-plate pass for this working from Carlisle as far as Blea Moor on a glorious June afternoon towards the end of steam and it turned out to be a never-forgotten experience—in more ways than one! It also showed just how much further steam traction could have been developed given the time, the technology and the will. In view of what is to follow, I suspect that it was the time and, most of all, the will that were lacking.

Nothing about these Long Meg trains was quite conventional and when I duly reported to the Loco Inspector's Office, tucked away under the mock gothic facade of Citadel's island platforms, I was welcomed by an Inspector who was obviously a character and looking forward to a happy afternoon in the hills. I had been warned that the Inspector to accompany me was one of the fastest things on wheels that Upperby had known for a long time. He also knew a great deal about the workings and the whims of steam loco-motives. "We've got a bit of a walk", I was informed, "He's stopping to pick us up at the Bog". I raised an eyebrow, as this was Carlisle and not the west of Ireland, but he was clearly a man who knew what he was about. So, clutching cameras and a borrowed Inspector's coat, I followed him manfully if a little nervously off the South end of the island platform at Citadel as the diesels moaned and wailed about us, tripped over a signal wire or two and vanished down the bank where the new power box now stands.

At the bottom of the bank was a junction, part of the complex of goods lines avoiding Citadel Station, and opposite was a signal box bearing the slightly improbable name of Bog Junction, a name it kept until it closed sometime in 1969. The Working Timetables, in a fit of prudery, called it Carlisle No 7 but to the men it was 'the Bog', no more, no less. While we waited for our chariot to appear, my companion reflected on the wartime conditions round Carlisle and recalled that on one occasion he had relieved a Midland crew off a goods train working north at Bog Junction and, eight hours later, had booked off again at Canal Junction just two miles to the north! I have no doubt that this was true, for Carlisle in the dark days of the early 1940s was a badly congested place.

In due course from under the bridge at the equally improbably named Rome Street Junction appeared No 92056, one of the 9F 2–10–0s with a single chimney, towing only a brake-van. Even at a first glance there was that indefinable something about this machine that picked her out as being in first class condition. Certainly she was not clean—no Kingmoor engines were towards the end of steam—but as she rolled to a stand there was steam only where there should be steam— a sizzling about the safety valves and wisps trailing from the injector. There was, in short, that quietness one associates with a

37

mechanically sound locomotive. The Inspector remarked to the effect that we were lucky to have a grand driver—although luck, as it later transpired, had little to do with it; organisation, more like, for the driver had been the Inspector's regular mate at Upperby for some years and also knew of only two regulator openings—wide or shut! The fireman likewise was young, strong and keen. The guard had that wary air of a man who knew we were up to something and didn't exactly like it, and even if he didn't start with a chip on his shoulder he certainly finished his shift with a bruise or two on his backside!

We climbed aboard to be most hospitably received, with much banter about how to run a train, and set sail for Long Meg sidings, sweeping under the LNWR main line, past Peterill Bridge where the old NER took fright and fled to Newcastle and the long demolished ghosts of Durranhill Sheds. If Derby Loco had known what was to follow,

Above: **Some idea of the long gradients and rugged terrain which face crews on the Settle and Carlisle line can be gained from this view of BR Standard 9F 2-10-0 No. 92012, which appears to be making very heavy going of the climb up to Ais Gill on August 25, 1966.**/*C. Lofthus*

there would have been ghosts in fact as well as fancy, for the League for the Prevention of Cruelty to Locomotives was destined to have a severe set-back before the afternoon was past! With the brakevan clattering behind us we ambled over the crossing at Low House and then tumbled into the glorious valley of the Eden about Armathwaite, the river glittering between the sunlit trees far below, shimmering with salmon. Through the two short tunnels at Barons Wood, past Lazonby and then a swing to the east across the Eden to a stop under the tree-lined scarp by Long Meg Quarry. A four-coupled 'Pug', once blue but now covered in many coats of grey anhydrite dust, was fussing about the quarry but our initial load of 10 hoppers was ready and we were soon on our way again with 92056 bestirring herself for the first time to confirm under load the impression that I had gained on the lazy loaf up the Eden Valley—this, for the last few months of steam, was a locomotive in very good mechanical condition. The next stop was New Biggin.

Of all the Settle and Carlisle line, the section from Carlisle to Appleby is probably the least known—people go to sleep or to dinner once they are off the high Pennines, and yet it is in many ways Sharland's masterpiece, for despite having less room to work in and more angry landowners to placate, this part of the line is every bit as fine as that up on the high fells. The contrast is absolute but the intention is the same—to produce a fast-running main line using every trick of the landscape. New Biggin was very much a part of this landscape—a secret station for a secluded village with some sidings kept in business only for yet more anhydrite. The station was a charming period piece in the best Midland Baroque tradition and on that June afternoon we had time to sample its beauties, for the 'Long Meg' was unceremoniously parked in the sidings to let the up 'Waverley' go by. It seems a long time ago now, but the Waverley Route from Edinburgh to Carlisle was still open then, and the lonely waits at Leeds were still in the future.

With the 'Waverley' out of section, we got the road and with a full load of 20 hoppers and a van we trundled out of New Biggin Sidings onto the main line. The 9F slipped, briefly but perceptibly, and there was more banter about the cab which I was to remember some ten miles on! So to Appleby, but with more than a hint of trouble brewing; first the exhaust steam injector played up, then its live steam counterpart. Unkind remarks from driver and fireman about Messrs Craven's contraptions were instantly corrected by the Inspector, who pointed out

Below: **18F! Another regular heavy job on the Settle and Carlisle in the last years of steam was this train of pre-assembled track; here 2-10-0s Nos 92125 and 92071 slog up towards Blea Moor on August 5, 1967.**/*C.J. Mills*

that when Cravens made them they worked—
it was only when the railways tried to make
them for themselves they didn't. We were
left to draw our own conclusions in an
atmosphere that would have made even a
television producer blush. Eventually, both
were persuaded to function after a fashion.

Appleby is the end of the sylvan reaches
of the Eden; ahead lie the great hills and
limestone scarps of the rather scraggy back-
bone of Northern England. While the driver
and fireman were watering No 92056, our
Inspector was doing yeoman work on those
cantankerous injectors—work, as far as a
layman could see, consisting of buckets of cold
water and the odd well-aimed but less than
gentle tap with the coal hammer. In about
10 minutes we were ready to leave. The
driver turned to me and said "I hear that
you've walked every inch of this road, Mr
Cross". I nodded in agreement. "Well,
you're driving from here to the top!", he
grinned. I muttered about Inspectors and
other such deterrents to unofficial driving
on BR metals, but back came a reply that
stopped me in my tracks. "We've got a shovel
for him as well—we're out to make express
times to Ais Gill, so you'd b— well better not
slip leaving here". The penny dropped with
the sickly thud of a dud coin found out—
this was a plot and I was an essential part of
it! I knew from frequenting Carlisle during
previous years that these Long Meg trains
were considered to be a challenge and that
likewise the 9Fs were considered to be the
best freight engines they had ever had. Now
my trip was being used as an excuse to find
out what they could do; what was to follow
owed nothing to my skill, but a great deal to
the designer of the 9Fs. We made Appleby
to Ais Gill with 640 tons in just over two
minutes of diesel express timings rated for
300 tons; it was a hectic half hour! I repeat
that I take no credit—I timorously did as I
was bid, but I knew the road, every inch of it,
and every signal post from the ivy-clad ones
about Griseburn to the high, exposed masts
of Mallerstang, their paintwork wracked and
tortured by the Helm Wind and the great

gales of the High Pennines. They may have
been hectic minutes, but they were minutes
never to be forgotten, for they must rank
among the all-time greats for power output
from a British steam locomotive.

By Settle and Carlisle standards, the start
southwards from Appleby is easy; a little less
than a mile at 1 in 440 until the line passes
under the main road from Penrith to the
east, followed by over a mile at 1 in 176
actually dropping into the valley of the Eden,
which is traversed by the Ormside Viaduct.
But beyond Ormside it is hard work right
to the top at Ais Gill. I got away from Appleby
without a trace of slip, opening the regulator
carefully on the gently rising grades past
the south box and the creamery and then
opening her up under the main road with
another turn on the reverser and a welcome
answer from 92056's exhaust. "Well at least
you didn't slip", conceded the driver, "But
you'll have to do a damned sight better than
that to keep express times to the Gill". I was
slightly taken aback, as I had rather fancied
my skill as a driver. "Now," said my mentor
"You've got a mile down to Ormside Viaduct and a mite of level across it—keep her
as she is until you're onto the viaduct and
then give her everything she'll take". As we
swung round the long curve to the south,
high above the wooded valley of the Eden, I
cautiously prepared to open the regulator a
trifle; "They big 9s like worked on full
regulator so give it all you can and a crack
with this hammer to make sure it stays that
way!" No half-measures for this driver; it
was briefly explained that regulators on 9Fs
had a habit of creeping shut. With that, the
driver thrust the coal hammer into my hands,
grabbed the third shovel and started
firing. As we swung onto the viaduct, the
Inspector looked back and gave me the
thumbs up and I gave that engine all she
would take. Our claustrophobic little world
seemed to surge forward with a shattering
roar; everything that could bang or rattle
banged and rattled like never before, but
92056 rode well. Only when I tried advanc-
ing the cut-off a little too far did she sit up

and dance. Up the first three miles at 1 in 100 we stormed, through the Helm Tunnel and past Griseburn Box nestling among its wind-tortured trees. Speed increased as the grade eased where the line passes high above the lovely isolated village of Crosby Garrett, with superb views of the Ranges to the north and its graceful viaduct set among the rooftops of the houses. Nine miles to go to the summit now, but most of this at 1 in 100 with only two short easings through Mallerstang and the station at Kirkby Stephen.

By Crosby Garrett 92056 was nicely warmed up with a white hot fire that was able to digest all that the three firemen could throw at it or, in the case of some of the bigger lumps, kick into it! We must have been holding a good 50 mph plus through Kirkby Stephen, with the exhaust so hot that it was 20 feet from the chimney top before it was even showing in the hot June afternoon air. At Kirkby what had so far been a thrilling experience became also a very personal one—my great friend Ivo Peters had been forced to temporarily foresake the Somerset & Dorset for a business trip to the North East and on his way home had arranged to photograph the 'Long Meg' at Kirkby Stephen the day I was to travel on it. We had met shortly before and his parting words were: "be sure and give me something worth taking." In the event I failed, because the fire and the weather were too hot for any spectacular smoke effects, but the buildup to his attempts had its humours.

The signalman at Kirkby Stephen shouted that the train was by Griseburn already, adding after a few seconds that it must be a diesel, for at this time Class 40s were used on the 'Long Meg' on odd occasions. Sound carried far on that still June day, and the exhaust of that 9F being thrashed flat out must have sounded very strange from three miles away! Only a couple of minutes later they were to realise from the smoke and noise that this was no diesel! The signalman left the railway shortly afterwards to take a job in Western Australia, but he assured me before he left that our antics that afternoon

had nothing to do with it! Ivo Peters had driven racing cars before the war and was made of sterner stuff; when told by the signalman, who knew both of us, that it was his mad so-and-so friend who was driving, he decided that he was going to Ais Gill to meet us. Thus began the Pennine equivalent of the Great Locomotive Chase. It can be done, as I know from personal experience, but it needs a very clear road and a train that is not out to break the all time record. It also needed the sheep of the upper Eden Valley to be in their pastures green abiding and not sprawled all over the narrow road! The sheep must have behaved that day, but on the locomotive all was not well, for shortly after passing Kirkby I saw some rude gestures from the Inspector to the official driver, and both crossed to the right hand side of the cab and peered down at the live steam injector. The Inspector came across to borrow the coal hammer as, with one eye on the track and the other on the efforts of the experts to get the reluctant injector to work again, I stormed 92056 up towards the Birkett Tunnel. Kicks, curses and blows from the hammer produced at least some slight flow of water to the boiler—and at our steaming rate, every little drop helped!

With the injector at least partially working again, the Inspector came across the cab twiddling pieces of cotton waste in his hands; my first reaction was that my driving had totally unnerved him but, above the roar of the exhaust and the cacophony of anything moveable in the cab, he managed to convey that the two twisted pieces of cotton waste that he now gave me were to be put in my ears in Birkett Tunnel. Now the Birkett Tunnel, though not very long, is cut from solid rock, and this reverberates far more than a brick-lined tunnel ever can. Even with our makeshift ear plugs the racket was tremendous, but far more alarming was the fact that the white-hot fire was flinging great flaming lumps of coal out of the chimney, and these were hitting the roof of the tunnel and bouncing back onto the tender and, even worse, through the open ventilator of the

cab roof. One well-aimed swipe from that invaluable coal hammer closed the ventilator and thereafter as far as I could see our rapidly dwindling stocks of coal were all burned in the firebox and not extraneously in the tender! Then suddenly daylight again and relative silence, a brief glimpse of Pendragon Castle ('ruins of', as the map would say) and a slight surge of speed as the grades eased for a mile to a modest 1 in 330 past Mallerstang Box. Nobody was talking much now; it was far too hot for one thing, and the firemen were getting fairly tired—all three of them! We were all worrying about those reluctant injectors, but 92056 was going

Left: **Even in latter years, the "Long Meg" trains were not the sole preserve of the 9Fs; here a grimy Stanier 8F 2-8-0 No. 48283 storms through Kirkby Stephen with loaded hoppers for Widnes on April 28, 1967.**/*Derek Cross*

Below: **On a fine day in late April 1967, BR Standard Class 9F 2-10-0 No. 92051 pounds away from Appleby with the afternoon Long Meg–Widnes train.**/*L. A. Nixon*

superbly well. It would have been a good Jubilee that could have made these times from Appleby with half the load. Above Mallerstang, the Settle and Carlisle hugs the eastern flank of Wild Boar Fell with the whole of Upper Edendale spread out beneath.

Then I saw it. Far below on that twisting mountain road, a large black Bentley going like a demented dormouse pursued by a thousand cats. I knew who it was and what he was after! The crew must have sensed my interest, for in turn they gave up coal heaving for a minute or two to peer over my shoulder. "Aye, that's the car that was in the yard at Kirkby—is it not your friends?" asked the driver. I nodded. "Christ, he's either crazy or can drive a car!" I assured them that he was competent at the latter art, though from our elevated position I began to wonder! Sheep scattered, curlews screamed and his passenger, a cleric of some renown, shut his eyes and, one must assume, prayed. As the cleric in question was something of an authority on church music, his prayers may have been in the doom-laden tones of Verdi's Requiem, but certainly he has never been near Westmorland since!

Still this was something of an insult to our crew—how dare anyone try and better them on a run like this! I was asked if I couldn't get another notch on the cut-off and was promptly evicted when I shook my head. The driver tried and may have got half a notch further; we were only a mile from the summit now and could afford to mortgage the boiler, as the rest of the journey to Blea Moor was, generally speaking, favourable to a southbound train. Added to which, the firebox had enough to keep it going to Ais Gill and beyond even at our fantastic steaming rate. For the first time in half an hour I relaxed and waited for the finale of the duel between 9F and Bentley. Like Wellington's description of the Battle of Waterloo it was 'a damned close run thing'. We were neck and neck abreast of the Ais Gill viaduct and I saw ahead of me two budding photographers leaning purposefully on the

road bridge half a mile north of Ais Gill loops. Their interest was focused on the roaring monster on the 'Long Meg' till, at the last second, they fled from the roaring monster of the Black Bentley bearing down sideways upon their backs! Ivo Peters won by a nose, as racing men would say.

Beyond Ais Gill things were more relaxed, and the crew decided that we had not done too badly, considering we had an inexperienced amateur driver and a Kingmoor Engine rather than an Upperby one—old rivalries round Carlisle died hard and the contempt of the LNWR shed for any of the others was absolute. As far as maintenance for hard running was concerned, it was probably with some justification.

It is a very strange thing about the Settle and Carlisle line that the most notorious lengths from the locomotive working point of view tend to be the most uninteresting scenically. The 'long drag' from Settle to Ribblehead has its moments, such as the view of Penygent from about Selside, or on the north side, the great vista northwards from Crosby Garrett, but these are only passing glimpses. The really great scenic stretches are in the Eden Valley, north of Appleby, and above all the views down Dentdale between Garsdale and Blea Moor Tunnel. This length of line across the great watershed of Northern England I have seen in all sorts of weather conditions and it never fails to fascinate. There is something of Tennyson's "On one side lay the ocean and on the other a great water" about it, for the moors around the Moorcock Inn drain three ways. The views down Dentdale that hot June afternoon were superb and the impression of the great viaducts of Arten Gill and Denthead from the footplate had to be seen to be appreciated. Such works of elegance in so bleak a surrounding have a very unreal quality, their airy improbability in marked contrast to the damp and smokey darkness of Blea Moor Tunnel immediately to the south.

After our hectic charge up to Ais Gill, this 10 miles were a pleasant relaxation. We had come up so swiftly that once the Long

43

Meg was safely parked in the loop at Blea Moor we all had time for tea and to examine the mightily-abused 92056. To my amazement, she was quite cool, with her safety valves simmering and still apparently game for anything. In due course the northbound empties appeared from across the curving viaduct behind another 9F, this time double-chimney No. 92249. We changed crews and set off back to Carlisle.

We had a pleasant if uneventful run back to Long Meg with the high country looking its best as the air cooled and the lowering sun etched out the crags and gullies of the Fells. There was no need for histrionics, for while 92249 was rougher than her elder southbound sister, with the odd knock here and there, she was more than equal to her task. As we bowled along, I began to think and draw lessons from that hectic half hour from Appleby to Ais Gill. With 640-odd tons on our tail we had run to the top in near enough express times calculated for a diesel with 300 tons less. Certainly the engine used had been specially selected, certainly we had a clear road, and certainly we had a set of very dedicated enthusiasts on the footplate, including the services of three firemen. Against this, I was an inexperienced driver, and while I knew every inch of the road and where to look out for signals, stiffening grades and the like, I certainly did not know the subtleties of the intricate art of driving a steam locomotive. Again, there were those bothersome injectors, which detracted from our performance, and the fact that this was a common user locomotive handled by many men on scores of duties.

The first two conclusions that I drew were the obvious ones—that the 9Fs had a very good boiler, and that their rugged construction allowed them to be thrashed mightily for long periods without any damage or overheating. My next was that such sustained power outputs are very labour intensive and thus very costly and only possible when there was an excuse for two extra men, as on the occasion of my Long Meg journey.

As we dropped back down the flanks of Wild Boar Fell, I recalled that the oil-fired Ka class locomotives of the New Zealand Railways were rated to haul 600 tons up nearly 19 miles of 1 in 50 from Oio to National Park on goods trains. Certainly the schedules were not nearly as fast as we had attempted on the 'Long Meg', but against this the grades were steeper and the curves more vicious with no superelevation on that very twisty single line, much of it among dripping trees. The gauge in New Zealand was only 3 ft 6 in, but while the oil-fired locomotives sometimes suffered from slipping, they were seldom short of steam. For some reason, although we have tried oil firing experiments in this country on several occasions, they have never been a success. Lack of experience I wonder, or lack of will? Not that this matters now, for despite the recent discovery of North Sea oil it would seem that this particular fuel will increasingly be at a premium. On the other hand, I mused, we do in Britain still have vast reserves of workable coal beneath our feet but due to resistance to modern methods of mining and very low production per man, back in the sixties, when oil was still cheap and plentiful, it was not considered economic to exploit our coal reserves. Certainly coal burnt to produce electricity is a more productive way of driving railway trains than steam locomotives could ever hope to be but diesels cannot use coal at all. Moreover, electrification requires such a massive long term investment, in some cases far more than the lines cost initially to build, that it is out of the question for many lines.

Such academic musings had to be forgotten that June evening as we dropped down the beautiful Eden Valley above Crosby Garrett with the ranges of Cross Fell to the northward. The great limestone and millstone grit escarpments of the northern Pennines are for cosmic reflection rather than day to day pedantic details. Yet the memory of this Long Meg trip won't go away. Why, if we had climbed the grades among these great hills so swiftly three hours before, was

Although most trains over the Settle & Carlisle, passenger or freight, involved some hard work, especially for the fireman, just occasionally some rather less strenuous, more pleasant jobs came along. On one such turn, Ivatt Class 2 2-6-0 No. 46426 canters through Appleby West with an inspection saloon./*Derek Cross*

the steam engine doomed? I don't claim to have the answer, for there are too many straws in the wind, and the winds which whip the High Pennines are mighty winds indeed.

We dropped our empties at Long Meg sidings and coasted down to Carlisle, the locomotive and van rocking round the curves of the lower Eden Valley in the golden sunlight of early evening. Then I was

saying my farewells and climbing that bank from Bog Junction back to Citadel and the train to Kilmarnock. A considerable amount of time behind schedule, a Class 47 regurgitated its noisome way under the arches of that great station, and I thought again. It is still too soon to judge in an unemotive way but I feel future generations may judge us harshly for our wholesale abandonment of steam before its full potential was realised especially at a time when the alternative fuel supplies were and are becoming increasingly finite.

"Who saw steam die?
I said the Accountant,
With myopic eye,
I saw steam die."

West of Swansea

Below: **The railways of the rural areas of Britain suffered most from Doctor Beeching's amputations in the 1960s, and those of West Wales were no exception. The Cardigan line has gone, as too has the line north from Carmarthen through Pencader and Lampeter to Aberystwyth, severing the westerly route to the north and, because of the parallel closure of the Cambrian line via Rhayader, forcing upon the residents of South and West Wales the final ignominy of having to travel via Shrewsbury (England!) to get to Aberystwyth and the remaining lines in North Wales. But at least the GW "main" line to Fishguard survives, mainly because of the Irish boat traffic, together with the lines down to Pembroke and here, at Milford Haven, where we find a Swindon three-car Cross Country set waiting to depart as the 17.05 to Swansea on August 8, 1966./R. E. Toop**

Above right: **Across the Daucleddau from Milford Haven and Neyland is Pembroke, served by a separate branch running east to the shores of Carmarthen Bay at Tenby before turning north to join the other lines at Whitland. And it is towards Whitland that 5700 Class 0-6-0PT No. 9748 is heading as she climbs away from the now-closed station at Templeton with the morning freight from Pembroke Dock in July 1963.**

Below right: **Lightweight load for a Manor this—No. 7815** *Fritwell Manor* **bowls along between Haverfordwest and Clarbeston Road with the morning train from Milford Haven to Carmarthen and, eventually, Paddington one day in July 1963.**

Like the Pembroke and Milford Haven lines, the Fishguard line has always been a single track. Nevertheless, it carries heavy traffic and was the regular stomping ground of many of the larger GW engines. Here (*Above left*) we see Hall class 4-6-0 No. 5905 *Knowsley Hall* making a vigorous ascent of the bank out of Fishguard with the 14.30 freight from Fishguard Harbour on a July day in 1963, while (*below left*) Castle class 4-6-0 No. 5097 *Sarum Castle* accelerates away from the Harbour station on August 25, 1962 with an afternoon boat train for London./*E. Thomas*

Above: Two Halls for two coaches—4-6-0 No. 5976 *Ashwicke Hall* pilots an unidentified sister engine on the climb out of Fishguard with a lightweight local to Clarbeston Road in July 1963.

Right: A typical rural Welsh railway scene that is regrettably no more—1600 Class 0-6-0PT No. 1648 simmers gently against the single platform at Cardigan soon after arrival with its single-coach 11.35 train from Whitland on August 21, 1962./*E. Thomas*

Above: **With two coaches and a bogie van to play with, GW 4500 Class 2-6-2T No. 4550 gallops away from the passing loop and station at Boncath with the 17.45 Cardigan–Whitland on July 31, 1959.**/*R. O. Tuck*

Left: **Nowadays, the line from Johnston to Neyland is closed to all traffic, but not so long ago, County class 4-6-0 No. 1027 *County of Stafford* was able to make this impressive start away from Whitland with the 14.40 Neyland–Paddington boasting six coaches.**/*G. T. Robinson*

Below: **The lines north and east from Carmarthen are now little more than a memory, although freight services as far as Lampeter on the truncated remains of the Aberystwyth line survived until comparatively recently. But before the cuts, on August 31, 1963, the Maesycrugiau signalman prepares to hand the single line staff for the next section to the north to the driver of BR Standard 2-6-2T No. 82003 at the head of the 14.55 from Carmarthen.**/*A. A. Vickers*

Right: **All services have now been withdrawn on the ex-LNW line east from Carmarthen across to the still open Swansea–Shrewsbury line at Llandilo, but before the demolition men came, 5700 Class 0-6-0PT No. 9632 was caught leaving Nantgaredig with the 9.50 Carmarthen–Llandilo on August 10, 1963.**/*G. T. Robinson*

Below: **"Felin Fach Station Signal Box" declares the nameboard on the somewhat less than impressive structure alongside Collett 7400 Class 0-6-0PT No. 7407 pauses at Felin Fach Halt to add a few more loaded milk tanks to the 11.45 Aberayron–Lampeter Milk train on July 31, 1959. The tanks will be forwarded to Carmarthen for onward transit to London the same evening.**/*R. O. Tuck*

Left: **Hall class 4-6-0 No. 6912** *Helmster Hall* **gets the distant on as she climbs away from Swansea around the Landore loop towards Cockett Tunnel on April 30, 1959 with the 13.50 Swansea–Carmarthen stopping train.**/*H. Daniel*

Right: **Hall class 4-6-0 No. 5905** *Knowsley Hall* **restarts a westbound parcels and mail train from Whitland on a fine day in the Summer of 1963.**/*G. T. Robinson*

Below: **Looking something of a refugee from the Valleys, 5600 Class 0-6-2T No. 6623 trundles a train of new sleepers through Cockett on the western approach to Swansea.**/*E. P. Gullis*

New Light on the Salisbury Disaster

J. T. HOWARD TURNER

At about 1.57 am on Friday, July 1, 1906, an up LSWR boat train derailed and overturned at high speed on the sharp curve at the east end of Salisbury Station. This much is well-known to railway historians. It has, however, always been a mystery why the driver, who knew the road well, took his train through the station at a speed which was bound to cause a derailment.

The train was conveying passengers off the liner ss *New York* that had arrived at Plymouth from America on the previous evening. It was running to a regular speed table, first used over two years earlier on Saturday, April 9, 1904, when the first of such trains was run for the American Line, in that case the ss *St Louis*. The speed table was reissued on April 21, 1904, to cover the running of the train for the ss *St Paul* on April 23, the only changes being the showing of certain additional intermediate passing times and the repetition of the instruction already issued by the Mechanical Engineer's Department on April 20 limiting the speed of trains passing non-stop through Salisbury to 30mph.

The main feature of these schedules was the elimination of one of the stops to change engines. Prior to the introduction of the boat-train timings, all passenger trains from the West had normally changed engines twice—at Exeter Queen Street (now Central) and at Salisbury, where all regular trains stopped in any case for traffic purposes, as they did in the down direction. The introduction of

tenders with larger water capacities in 1897 had, however, enabled longer non-stop runs to be made without difficulty—the LSWR never had any water troughs. With limited loads, the introduction of a schedule which divided the run from Devonport to Waterloo into two stages only became practicable for the first time. A convenient half-way point was Templecombe, some $117\frac{1}{2}$ miles from Devonport and just over 112 miles from Waterloo; moreover, by making the engine-change at the up home signal at Templecombe, the passengers got the benefit of an undisturbed rest after joining the train at Stonehouse Pool until they reached Waterloo. An allowance of three minutes was shown at Templecombe for changing engines, but otherwise the boat-train timing was generally similar to that of the ordinary express trains, which had been accelerated earlier and their timings proved by a trial trip. Hence, it was felt that there was no need for a trial trip of the boat-train timing.

The timings were, of course, issued by the Superintendent of the Line. In addition, however, the Chief Mechanical Engineer's Office issued a notice dated May 3, 1904, stating that the Devonport Boat Special must be run to scheduled time in future, and followed this by another, dated June 14, 1904, worded as follows:

"On 3rd May, I requested that this train should be run to scheduled timings.

Any driver, running it at higher than scheduled speed, will be taken off his engine (*By Order*).

This notice is to be posted on the NOTICE BOARD at .... Station, and Foreman are to call the attention of Enginemen and Firemen to the instructions and arrangements therein specified, and take their signatures for same in Notice Book, and they are immediately to report all cases of neglect or departure therefrom."

The undoubted implication was that drivers had been gaining time by running faster than normal with this train! No further notices were issued by the CME's Office, and no record is available of the number of men taken off their engines for this offence; it is likely, however, that under the rigid discipline enforced at this time there would have been very few offenders.

Nevertheless there was a case early in 1906 of a private special train—not the boat train —being reported to the Superintendent of the Line's Office by the Engineer's Department as having run through Salisbury at over 30mph. Henry Holmes, then Superintendent of the Line, stated at the Board of Trade Inquiry into the Salisbury Accident that this incident caused the boat-train timing to be revised and reissued on February 10, 1906. The adjustments were small but one of these was important—the insertion of passing times for Salisbury West and East signalboxes. One minute was allowed for this section, and as the boxes were, and still are, 755 yards apart the permitted speed was between 25 and 26mph. The timing allowed one further minute from the East box to Tunnel Junction, a distance of 1,519 yards, requiring an average speed of about 48mph.

The other alterations to the timing included a tightening by one minute between Coleford Junction and Exeter St David's so as to give a passing time one minute earlier at Yeovil Junction, followed by an easing of two minutes on to Templecombe so as to give an arrival time there one minute later than hitherto. With the same three minute stop at Templecombe up home signal, departure from there was thus one minute later than previously, and this alteration remained to Dinton. The passing time at Salisbury was, as already stated, replaced by bookings for the West and East boxes, one minute apart; the West box timing was one minute later than the previous time for the station itself, connoting a further slight slowing, and the Andover Junction time was two minutes later than hitherto. No change was made on to Basingstoke, but one minute was taken out of the allowance to Woking and another on to Hampton Court Junction, so that the timing to that point (4 hrs 4 min)

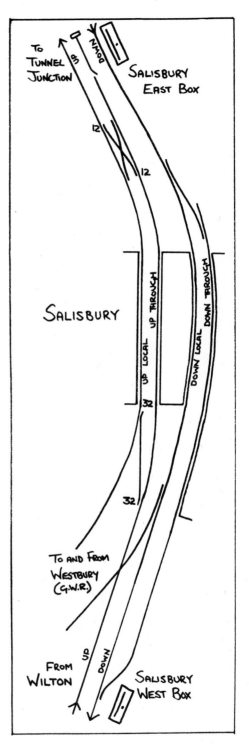

The two up lines through Salisbury: Battle of Britain class 4-6-2 No. 34059 *Sir Archibald Sinclair* leaves Salisbury (*left*) on the Up Through Line with the 8.20 Plymouth Friary–Waterloo on August 31, 1958 and swings through the reverse curves of Salisbury East No. 12 crossover onto the Up Line to Tunnel Junction. In contrast (*below right*), Q1 class 0-6-0 No. 33023 restarts a Swansea–Bournemouth train away from Salisbury on the Up Local on July 23, 1960. As can be seen, although the curve out of the platforms on the Up Local is marginally sharper, the reverse curve through the scissors crossover in the foreground is avoided./K. L. Cook, R. A. Panting

was the same as previously, as was the arrival time at Waterloo, 4 hrs 20 min for the 229½ miles.

Apart from the tightening-up west of Exeter so as to give a one minute earlier passing time at St Davids, which may have been to draw attention to the need for right-time working over the GWR in that area, and the insertion of what would now be called a recovery margin approaching Templecombe, the main change was, as indicated by Henry Holmes, to emphasise the 30mph limit through Salisbury station. However, the subsequent allowance of only one minute between Salisbury East and Tunnel Junction boxes, calling for an average of about 48mph immediately after the 25–26mph timing from Salisbury West to Salisbury East, was a virtual impossibility.

In the working timetables for the period from June 1 to September 30, 1906, the specific timing for the boat express at

Salisbury East box was omitted, but two minutes were still allowed for the distance between the West and Tunnel Junction boxes, 2,274 yards apart—an average of 38.7mph. Major J. W. Pringle, the Board of Trade Inspecting Officer, stated in his report on the accident that "This is not at variance with the speed restriction of 30mph through the station, or with the one minute timing between the East box and the West box."

The Author considers that the East box timing was dropped because strict compliance both with it and the Tunnel Junction timing was impossible, but the elimination of the intermediate timing must have resulted in drivers passing the East box a little earlier than hitherto in order to avoid being late by Tunnel Junction—in other words, it had the unfortunate result of militating against the 30mph restriction through the station.

Because the boat train timing was very little different from that of the ordinary express trains, no special men were detailed for the duty; any express driver whose turn it was worked the boat-train. According to F. C. French, who was Outdoor Assistant to the CME, in evidence to the BOT Inquiry into the Salisbury Accident, during the $2\frac{1}{4}$ years from the date when the first boat-train was run, up to the time of the accident, some 30 drivers had worked it—some once only, others twice, and others up to a maximum of nine or ten times.

The conclusion from the foregoing can only be that, from the Company's standpoint there was nothing special about the timing or working of the train, which ran weekly when required.

Through Salisbury station there were, and still are, two Up roads, the Up Local (with platform on the left) on the outside and the Up Through on the inside, beyond which is an island platform, the other face of which serves the Down Local; the Down Through is beyond this and has its own separate platform on the south side of that line, as shown in the attached diagram. The Board of Trade Accident Report is in error in its Plan A, the titles of the Down lines being transposed thereon.

The line from Wilton to Salisbury approaches the latter on a falling gradient of 1 in 115, which eases to 1 in 183 about half a mile before Salisbury station. According to the LSWR Gradient Manual of 1887 and to the LSWR Diagram of the System (undated, but shortly before the Grouping), the line was level through the station, but according to Plan A of the Accident Report there was a

fall of 1 in 520 from the West box to the West end of the island platform and a rise of 1 in 547 along the length of that platform, succeeded by a short rise of 1 in 158 before becoming level. No doubt these were all averaged out to level for the purpose of compiling the Gradient Manual and the Diagram of the System. At the top of the 1 in 115 falling gradient the alignment, which has been straight after leaving the curves at Wilton, enters a compound right-hand curve starting at 100 chains radius and finishing at 200 chains. This is followed by a short section of straight and then by a further right-hand curve of 150 chains radius. This, without any intermediate straight, runs into a 75 chains left-hand curve which finishes just before entering Salisbury station. There is then a short length of 18 chains curve to the left, followed by a straight beside the up platforms. There is next a compound left-hand curve some 92 yards long at about 12 chains at either end and at 8 chains over the greater part of its length. The diagram of the System averages this out to 10 chains throughout, which was the curvature when it was a circular curve, only, prior to realignment.

At the end of this curve, the Up Local line continues straight towards Tunnel Junction and London, while the Up Through leads into a dead-end road known as the Middle (or Engine) Siding, a left-hand facing turnout leading across to the Up Local line—which now becomes the Up line—the latter being joined by a trailing connection which is curved to the right in the normal direction of running off the Up Through line. A facing connection from the Up Local to the Middle Siding runs across the connection from the Up Through to the Up line, the whole layout thus forming a scissors crossover which trains on the Up Through line have to pass through before joining the Up road towards Tunnel Junction and Waterloo. The radius of each part of this scissors crossover used by Up Through line trains, and operated by No 12 slide in Salisbury East box, was about $7\frac{1}{2}$ chains.

There was no cant on the Up Through line

at the commencement of the compound curve but it was built up rapidly, being $1\frac{1}{8}$ in 10 yd after the curve commenced and $3\frac{1}{2}$ in at 20 yds. This height was maintained for about 15 yd, and was then gradually reduced to $2\frac{1}{8}$in 10yd before the east end of the curve. A check rail was provided, starting 10yd from the commencement of the curve (where the cant was $1\frac{1}{8}$in) to 10yd from its end (cant $2\frac{1}{8}$in). There was, of course, no cant through the scissors crossover. After the scissors crossover, the line continues level for a short distance and then rises at 1 in 305, later easing to 1 in 610.

Since 1906, modifications to the permanent way have been made which have resulted in the radii of certain connections being different from those quoted above. For example, the minimum radius of the Up Through to Up line connection forming part of the scissors crossover at the east end of the station is now 577 feet, about 8.7 chains, instead of about $7\frac{1}{2}$ chains. At present, the turnout to the Up Local at the west end of the station has a radius of 613 feet, about 9.3 chains, and a switch radius of 488.6ft, about 7.4 chains; it was probably little different in 1906.

Certain of the boat-trains run prior to the accident are known to have been worked by class T9 4-4-0 engines. Some of this class had six-wheeled tenders, but others had the big bogie tenders with increased water capacity. It is almost certain, as previously indicated, that the engines used on non-stop runs from Templecombe to Waterloo were fitted with bogie tenders. The train involved in the accident was worked from Templecombe by a class L12 4-4-0, which had a bogie tender similar in design to those attached to some of the T9s. The only difference between the two classes which could be considered a significant factor in the train working under discussion was the height of the boiler centre-line—it was 7ft 9in on the T9s, and 8ft 3in on the L12s. The height of the centre of gravity of the L12 class was calculated by the CMEs Office to be 5ft, but the Inspecting Officer felt that this was on the low side. In the absence of any figures to the contrary, I consider that it might be reasonable to assess the centre of gravity of the L12 as 5ft 3in above rail level, and that of the T9 as 4ft 9in. Merchant Navy class engines have been worked non-stop through Salisbury station on numerous occasions in connection with the former 'Devon Belle' and also on occasional special trains; again, in the absence of any official SR records, I consider the height of their centre of gravity might be taken as 5ft 9in. The attached Table shows the calculated overturning speeds for these three classes of engine with their centre of gravity assumed as above, on curves of various radii. The reverse-curve effect through No 12 crossover would cause the derailing speeds to be lower than those shown for a single turnout. The addition of cant would raise the overturning figures for the Up Through line east of the platforms—the Inspecting Officer put the latter figure as 67–68mph for class L12.

The first point to note is that the overturning speeds of all three classes of engine are very similar, and hence that the effect of the height of the boiler centre and the centre of gravity is not really significant. The second point to note is that the speeds shown in the Table are only about twice the permitted maximum speed of the 1904–06 era; this in itself shows clearly that the official speed limit was far too high, bearing in mind that the locomotives concerned were not provided with speedometers.

Some years ago I was on the footplate of a Merchant Navy class engine which was taken through a facing crossover of about 9.3 chains radius from one road to the next at 22mph by the speedometer (subsequently found to be about 3mph slow) and was able to observe at first hand the very rough riding and the heavy lurch and roll as the engine recovered from the first half of the curve and ran into the second half. The overturning speed for a single turnout of 9.3 chains radius for this class of engine, assuming the centre of gravity to be 5ft 9in, would be about 61mph, but the derailing speed on a crossover might well be

as low as 50 mph. It has already been shown that variations in the height of the centre of gravity do not have a very significant effect, so that it may be assumed that similar speeds would have produced similar results with the T9 and L12 classes. Whilst a speed of 25mph in this instance was certainly not dangerous, the successive rolls of the engine from one side to the other, combined with the lurching, were such that no crew in their senses would have run the engine at a much higher speed through such a connection; at 30–35mph the riding would have been very rough indeed, and any speed above that could certainly be classed as dangerous. Since the radii of the No 12 connections at Salisbury East were 7½ chains instead of 9.3 chains, a speed of even 30mph through that connection could almost be classed as dangerous—yet this was the permitted maximum speed at the time of the accident. It is important to note that it is the second, reverse curve which is the cause of the trouble in crossovers, in that the reduction of weight on the inner rail of the first curve due to excessive speed can be the cause of derailment due to flange-climbing when the inner rail of the first curve becomes the outer rail of the second, reverse curve before the engine has had an opportunity to recover from the roll of the first curve and begins to roll over the other way.

By similar reasoning, the overturning speed for the turnout from the Up line to the Up Local at Salisbury West would have been about 57–63mph for the L12 and 60–66mph for the T9, based on the existing switch radius of approximately 7.4 chains and the turnout radius of approximately 9.3 chains—on average, just over 60mph for the T9 and a little less for the L12. These speeds are slightly lower than those applying to the compound curve at the east end of the station when allowance is made for the cant on the latter, but a train running over the Up Local line would not have to negotiate the reverse curves through No 12 crossover as it came off the Up Through at the east end, where, as we have seen, an even lower speed would cause derailment. In other words, it

A telephoto lens makes the curves at the east end of Salisbury seem even sharper as Rebuilt Battle of Britain class Pacific No. 34088 213 *Squadron* **waits in the wet for the Up Through starting signal with a stopping train for Waterloo on April 21, 1964.**/*P. H. Wells*

would have been better if non-stopping trains through Salisbury had been run via the Up Local line, rather than via the Up Through.

Although the technical considerations discussed here would not have been known to footplate staff of the era, very little practical experience of running through connections and around curves would be necessary to establish the basic facts in their minds. It was undoubtedly this sort of experience that prompted the Chief Mechanical Engineer's Office at Nine Elms to issue the instruction on April 20, 1904, that the maximum speed of non-stopping trains passing through Salisbury was not to exceed 30mph; unfortunately this limit, based on rule of thumb rather than

fact, was much too high and, as we have seen, could almost be classed as dangerous when applied to the No 12 connections at Salisbury East. Other express drivers who had driven the boat-train are on record in the Accident Report as giving their opinion that "an express driver, even on the first occasion of his running through Salisbury without stopping, would recognise that it was necessary to slacken speed at the east end of the station, on account of the sharp curve."

It has to be remembered that the LSWR Working Timetable specifically showed the boat trains as being run via the Through Line and any official deviation would have been noted; on the other hand, there have been many recorded instances of local wisdom, especially among Signalmen, giving rise to unofficial variations, and these tend not to be recorded, especially at night!

It has already been demonstrated that it would have been preferable for non-stopping trains to have been put up the Local line instead of up the Through. Although no evidence is available to show that any of the boat-trains operated before that involved in the accident were, in fact, run via the Up Local line, if this had been the case, it might well be a reason for the driver's otherwise inexplicable behaviour that fatal night.

The late Charles Rous-Marten, writing in the *Railway Magazine* in 1904, says that boat-trains had been run through Salisbury station behind T9 class engines at high speed, and after the accident in 1906, he claimed that on one occasion the speed was still 60mph at Tunnel Junction—after running through the station and travelling about ¾ mile up a gradient commencing at 1 in 305 and later easing to 1 in 610. In view of the figures already given, it is clear that Rous-Marten's estimates of speed must have been very wide of the mark, since the overturning speed of the T9s would have been little more than 60mph even if run on the Up Local line. However, I do not think that it is impossible that a really hard-bitten crew might have taken a train through the Up Local line at perhaps 40mph; I very much doubt, however if even they would have done it on the Up Through!

If such a foolish action had been taken, though, it is almost certain that the result would have discouraged the driver and fireman from doing anything like it again, quite apart from the blatant disregard of the relevant instructions from the CMEs Office. Incidentally, the fact that the instruction limited speed to 30mph suggests that prior to its issue, an attempt had been made to negotiate Salisbury at a considerably higher speed, and not merely at, say 35mph. If this be accepted, it lends credence to the possibility of earlier runs having sometimes, at any rate, been routed via the Up Local line.

Driver W. J. Robins, who had charge of No 421 on the night of the accident, was 40 years old, and had had 22 years' service with the LSWR. He had been a fireman for eight years, working between Exmouth Junction and Salisbury, and when he was 32 was promoted to driver at Nine Elms, driving

between London and Exeter for the next eight years until the accident. He undoubtedly knew the road very well, and was a teetotaller. It was, however, his first trip with the boat-train. His fireman, Arthur Gadd, was 29 years old, and had had 12 years' service with the Company, the last eight as a fireman.

On this occasion the boat-train left Devonport at 11.01pm on June 30, and was thus due to arrive at Templecombe at 1.23am and to depart at 1.26am. It in fact arrived there one minute early, and left on time. Guard Harrison, who had had 29 years' service with the Company, admitted at the Inquiry that he had omitted to make a brake test after the engine change, and also that he had not made one before leaving Devonport. However, he stated that there were 18–19in of vacuum on starting from Devonport and that he saw the vacuum fall at Exeter St David's, where there was a stop for signals, and at Templecombe, as well as slightly at other points. The train, consisting five bogie vehicles weighing 113 tons tare, left Templecombe on schedule at 1.26am, but immediately began to lose time. Despite the fact that the start from Templecombe in the up direction is downhill at 1 in 80 for a mile, followed by an easing to 1 in 160 for a short distance and a mile of level before the switchback at 1 in 90 to 1 in 100 on to Gillingham commences, the average start-to-pass speed for the 6¾ miles to Gillingham was less than 43mph. Up the rise ranging from 1 in 130 to 1 in 100 on to Semley, just over 4 miles, the pass-to-pass average was only 45½mph. But on to Tisbury, almost 5 miles further and largely downhill at 1 in 270, the average rose to nearly 60mph, while the length of 4¼ miles on to Dinton, again mainly on gentle falling gradients, was covered at over 64mph. Dinton to Wilton, 5¾ miles, and an average little more than level with a slight rise balancing a fall, was covered at 70mph. Despite the acceleration, however, the train was now four minutes late and it is clear that Robins, whatever the reason for his poor running up to Semley, was now doing his best to regain time. The timing from

Wilton to Salisbury West box allowed $3\frac{1}{2}$ minutes, but Robins did it in two and was now only two minutes late.

According to Guard Harrison, it was the usual practice with the boat train—until February 1906—for the drivers to start to brake just before reaching the west end of the platform, the speed then being "about 50mph", so as to round the curve at the east end "at 30–40mph". We have already seen that such a speed at the east end of the station could be considered dangerous. Harrison went on to say in his evidence that after the Notice giving separate passing times for the West and East signal boxes was issued in February 1906, the practice "has been to reduce the speed considerably more. The brakes would generally be applied about the West box, the speed at the west end of the platform would be generally about 30mph, and about the same speed through the east end of the station; the brakes would be generally kept applied until the East box was reached." Harrison then said that on the night of the accident the brakes were not applied by the driver at the West box nor at any point in the station, and the Inspecting Officer concluded that the speed of the train when it became derailed was at least 60mph and possibly as much as 70mph. Harrison, recalled for further questioning, stated that he had not made an emergency application of the brake, despite the fact that he recognised that the speed approaching the west end of the station was unsafe, because he was "afraid that with steam applied and at high speed, there would be a danger of a coupling breaking, or other damage being done to the train . . ."; he thought that he could attract the driver's attention in sufficient time by gently applying first the hand and then the vacuum brake.

The theory has sometimes been advanced that the regulator of No. 421 had jammed open, and that both men on the engine were preoccupied in trying to close it. Signalman Mundy, on duty in the West box, stated that "steam was shut off when the train passed my box"; it seems that he meant that steam was shut off only as the train passed

his box, and not that the train passed it with steam already shut off. After the accident, the engine was found with the regulator closed, the reverser within an inch of full forward gear, and the brake handle in the running (off) position. If Robins had indeed suffered a jammed regulator, had concentrated on getting it shut, and had only succeeded in so doing as he passed the West box, there was still plenty of time for him to have made an emergency brake application. Furthermore, there was nothing to stop him applying the brake while trying to shut the regulator—the light train would of course have resulted in a long stopping distance, but it would have considerably reduced speed. However, it is clear that Robins never applied the brake at all, so it would seem that the jammed regulator theory is irrelevant.

My great friend, the late Pelham Maitland, felt that a contributory factor to Robins' undoubted responsibility for the derailment may have been leakage of water around the pin of the leading bogie of the tender, causing that bogie to be stiff in turning. Mr Maitland, before he retired, was Running Shed Superintendent at Nine Elms and knew the T9 and L12 classes intimately. The design was apparently such that it was very difficult to stop leakage, since the bogie pin was secured under the front part of the tank where the head-room was extremely limited. Whilst one has to recognise that this may have been a contributory factor, I do not think that, at the speed the train was undoubtedly travelling, it was of major importance.

I have tried to set out all the factors which may in any way have been significant in this accident. Whilst there may be circumstances connected with the working of the train—for example, the reason for the poor start from Templecombe, resulting in four minutes being lost to Wilton—which remain unexplained, I am convinced that, on the falling gradients from Wilton, Driver Robins was running as hard as he could in order to regain lost time, and that he thought he could get away with a fast run

SITUATION AND RADIUS	CALCULATED OVERTURNING SPEEDS (mph)			SPEED LIMITS (mph)	
	T9 class (*4ft 9in**)	*L12 class* (*5ft 3in**)	*MN class* (*5ft 9in**)	1904–06	1973
Salisbury West Up line to Up Local turnout (No 32) (7.4 chains approx)	60	57	55	30	10
Salisbury East Up Through line east of platforms (8 chains minimum)	62½†	59½‡	57½§	30	10
Salisbury East Up Through to Up line crossover (No 12) (7½ chains, reverse curves)	60¶	¶57	55¶	30	10

* Estimated centre of gravity.
† Probably about 70mph with cant as provided in 1906.
‡ Probably about 67mph with cant as provided in 1906.
§ Probably about 65mph with cant as provided in 1906.
¶Calculated overturning speed for single turnout; the overturning speed through the reverse curves of a crossover would certainly be considerably less.

through Salisbury in order to regain further time. It could be that Robins had previously worked some other (non-boat) train non-stop through Salisbury on the Up Local line, and did not realise that the Salisbury East No 12 crossover was a veritable death-trap awaiting any really high speed run on the Up Through line. The fact that he did not brake at all seems conclusive evidence that he thought that by not doing so he would be doing no more than breaking the official speed limit. He badly miscalculated, however, how fast his engine could travel round the east-end curve; even if his train had negotiated this, however, with most unpleasant results for the passengers as well as for the footplate crew themselves, a derailment would still seem to have been inescapable over the reverse curves of No 12 scissors crossover.

Up to the time of the accident, the LSWR route to Plymouth was shorter than that of the GWR whose route lay through Bristol. Subsequently, the GWR opened its direct route via Westbury to through traffic, bringing the distance from Paddington to Plymouth below that from Waterloo. The arrangement between the two companies was that the LSWR carried the passengers and the GWR carried the mails—their route via Bristol was very convenient for mail traffic to the Midlands. After the Salisbury accident, the LSWR abandoned non-stop running through the station; this was probably covered by a local instruction, for it was certainly not referred to in the Appendix dated January 1, 1911, although the rule that all trains must stop at Salisbury was included, on page 88 of the Appendix dated July 25,

1921. The boat-train continued to run via the LSWR until May 1910, but after 1906 stopped at Exeter and Salisbury.

Major (later Colonel) Pringle inquired into the accident, and made a point of saying, in his Report dated July 31, 1906, that the east-end curve, even if negotiated at the permitted 30mph, "Would mean discomfort in travelling and possibly cause alarm in the minds of passengers". Increase in the cant on the curve did not appear to be possible, and in any case would be somewhat pointless, as the immediately following No 12 connections could not have any appreciable cant. Pringle therefore recommended that the east-end curves should have a maximum speed limit of 15 mph. He also thought that consideration should be given to the advisability of keeping both the Up and Down distant signals on, "with the object of emphasising the speed limits". With the cessation of non-stop running through Salisbury, there was no immediate need to lay down any speed limits, and indeed the first publication of these that I can trace appeared on May 9, 1947, in Supplement No 1 to the book of Permanent Speed Restrictions effective from October 1, 1945. The figure laid down was 10mph on all roads, this action clearly being taken in preparation for the renewal of non-stop running through Salisbury when the 'Devon Belle' service began on June 20, 1947. This limit of 10mph is still in force.

When the T9 class engines were introduced they were found to be very powerful and fast, and in the hands of the more enterprising crews they made some good runs. A few of the men undoubtedly began to get into the practice of running fast round curves, and this habit was, I feel sure, a factor of importance in the Salisbury accident. Even in later years, instances of running at far too high a speed around curves were not unknown. The most extreme instance that I can personally recall took place on Christmas Eve, 1930, when an up train from Southampton, consisting of nine non-corridor bogies headed by T9 class 4-4-0 No E305, was taken through Clapham Junction on the then Up Main Through line (what is now the Down Main Through) at a speed of about 70mph. This curve is nowadays of 19 chains radius, with a cant of 4in; due to the limitations of the station platforms, it was almost certainly similarly laid out in 1930. The speed limit was then, and still is, 40mph; the overturning speed could not have been much higher than 80mph, and I can still, in my mind's eye, see the locomotive and vehicles *heeling slightly outwards* and the last vehicle swaying violently. It is no exaggeration to say that it was very nearly a repetition of the Salisbury accident, over 24 years before; I certainly have no desire whatsoever to see anything remotely like it again.

Lincolnshire Lines

Right: **Now completely closed, the ex-GN line from Bourne to Sleaford eked out its final years with a twice-weekly freight as far as Billingborough; here 204hp diesel shunter No. D2027 shunts the yard at Rippingale in pouring rain on September 28, 1962.**/*A. Moyes*

Below: **Then still almost new, the penultimate Thompson class B1 4-6-0, No. 61408, restarts a York–Colchester train away from Lincoln Central on February 23, 1952.**/*J. Cupit*

Above: **Raven NER B16/1 class 4-6-0 No. 61434 wheels a heavy coal train across the fens towards March on the ex-GN&GE Joint Line near Gosberton on September 30, 1961.**/*M. J. Esau*

Left: **Under the footbridge at Lincoln Central comes WD class 2-8-0 No. 90031 with an eastbound freight on June 20, 1960.**/*D. C. Ovenden*

Below: **Further south on the GN & GE Joint line, on the border with Cambridgeshire, was the now-closed station at French Drove. Class V2 2-6-2 No. 60889 calls in May 1961 with a Doncaster–March local.**/*M. J. Esau*

Right: **Much of North Lincolnshire was once the province of the Great Central, and Barnetby was an important junction in the system. Here, B1 class 4-6-0 No. 61405 arrives with a New Holland–Lincoln train on a wintry day in the mid-1950s.**/*R. E. Vincent.*

Below: **In contrast, the lines of East Lincolnshire were the exclusive province of the Great Northern. Now, many of the lines are closed to all traffic; one comparatively recent casualty was the line north from Firsby through Louth to Grimsby, together with the remainder of the coastal loop to Mablethorpe. On August 13, 1965, a Derby twin diesel unit waits at Mablethorpe to depart on the nine-mile trip to the junction with the main line at Willoughby.**/*J. Cupit*

Left: Long into BR days—indeed, in many cases, until closure in the early 1970s—the East Lincolnshire lines retained much of their pre-Grouping atmosphere, including many GN somersault signals. Firsby was no exception; before the advent of diesel multiple-units, B1 class 4-6-0 No. 61391 arrives from the south with a Boston–Grimsby stopping train./*J. Cupit*

Right: In early BR days, before the northern part of the coastal loop to Mablethorpe was closed, Ivatt GNR class C12 4-4-2T No. 67379 awaits departure from Louth with a loop train to Willoughby./*J. Cupit*

Below: Nowadays, Skegness is one of the few Lincolnshire coastal resorts to retain its passenger services. Back in 1961, with the GN influence still very evident in the signals, signalbox and coaching stock, B1 class 4-6-0 No. 61406 sets out with the 9.38 to Kings Cross on September 2./*E. T. Gill*

Above left: **Scenes at Spalding: Until the diesels came, the B1 class 4-6-0s were the mainstay of Lincolnshire passenger and parcels motive power. No. 61250** *A. Harold Bibby* **accelerates away towards Peterborough** (*left*) **with an up Grimsby parcels on August 21, 1964**

Below left: **One of H. G. Ivatt's LMS Class 4F 2-6-0s, No. 43014, finds itself treading ground familiar to its Great Northern predecessors from the drawing board of H. A. Ivatt** (*below*) **as it wheels a lengthy GN & GE Joint line freight south through Spalding for March on June 24, 1958.**

Gresley's O2 class 2-8-0s performed much useful work on heavy GN & GE line freights, and were a common sight at Spalding, A pristine O2/3 No. 63949 heads for Whitemoor Yard (*above right*) **with a heavy coal train from the north on August 5, 1953, while sister engine No. 63971** (*below right*) **takes the down through freight line on October 12, 1957 with a northbound mixed freight.**/*P. H. Wells (3)*, *A. R. Carpenter*

Type 1s in tandem—two BTH 800hp type 1 Bo-Bos, Nos D8231 and D8232, approach Welwyn Garden City with the 6.33 Ashburton Grove–Blackbridge Tip rubbish train on April 11, 1968./*D. L. Percival*

Diesels Defunct

DAVID PERCIVAL

At the end of 1967, Class 5s, 8Fs, "Britannias" and 9Fs were still going strong in the North West of England—and one class of main-line diesel, the original North British-built "Warship", became extinct. Because we were preparing to mourn the passing of the steam engine, nobody cared.

Five years or so later, appeals for funds were still being made by hopeful preservationists for this or that steam locomotive—and one of the Swindon-built "Warships" became the first main-line diesel to be preserved. Somebody cared!

Clearly, the diesel has established a place in British railway history, and it has made an impression on the railway enthusiast. The word 'history' is by no means out of place in relation to this modern form of traction; a dozen of the main-line diesel classes built for British Railways since the late 1950s have already been withdrawn from service. Indeed, if the original 'pilot' scheme had continued as planned, even more may have shared the same fate.

The plan was to compare various classes of diesel locomotive—built in small quantities at BR workshops and by outside contractors—and choose one in each power range for large-scale construction. Thus there may by now have been perhaps only half-a-dozen classes in service. Different types were to be tried out at various depots and compared in day-to-day service, but it was soon realised that diesel and steam locomotives are not happy stable-mates, and the maintenance problems resulting from odd diesels scattered around the country were too enormous to contemplate. In addition, recruitment of staff to service steam engines was becoming increasingly difficult.

So it was decided that dieselisation must go ahead as rapidly as possible. Many more examples of some of the 'prototype' diesels were ordered before any long-term trials had been completed. Inevitably, some were successful, others less so. The classes already withdrawn have generally been the less successful types and the non-standard types which were never built in any great quantity. I have my own opinions about the category into which each class should be placed, but I am keeping them to myself. However, one cannot but wonder if it is significant that all the classes built by the North British Locomotive Company have disappeared!

The first class to disappear entirely was, as already mentioned, the original A1A–A1A "Warship". Five were built by the North British Locomotive Company and the first, No. D600 *Active*, was the Western Region's first main-line diesel, early in 1958. It featured hydraulic transmission, as did all that Region's big diesels until the English Electric Type 3s appeared in South Wales five years later. I remember seeing *Active* at Paddington when it was just a few months old, waiting to leave with the "Royal Duchy". In the adjacent platforms were a "King" and the gas-turbine No. 18000, once thought to be a serious rival to the steam engine. Of these three forms of express motive power, steam has gone, diesel-hydraulic was destined to follow shortly afterwards and, strangely, the gas-turbine was to re-appear in the Advanced Passenger Train—but this seems unlikely now.

Swindon's version of the "Warship", comprising Nos. D800–32/66–70, was built during 1958–61. These were more powerful but smaller machines with four-wheeled bogies, and fully justified the claim that hydraulic transmission resulted in a lighter locomotive than a similarly-powered diesel-electric with its generator equipment. So, for its next batch of "Warships", Nos. D833–65,

North British adopted the Swindon design. Both classes could be seen on all Western Region main lines, hauling everything from china clay trains to the "Bristolian". For some years they also hauled Waterloo-Exeter expresses. Maroon livery was applied from 1963 onwards, until BR blue became standard, so many members of the class appeared in green, maroon and blue during their careers.

Simultaneous withdrawal of Nos. D600-4 took place at the end of 1967 and the later versions were withdrawn between August 1968 and December 1972.

Perhaps the most unusual of the 'pilot' scheme diesels was the Metropolitan-Vickers 1,200 hp Co-Bo, with one six-wheel and one four-wheel bogie. Twenty were built, Nos. D5700-19, and they were set to work on the Midland main line, often working in pairs—particularly on St. Pancras-Manchester expresses and the overnight London-Glasgow "Condor" express freight service. Their

Crossley engine was a two-stroke diesel with exhaust pulse pressure-charging—another unorthodox feature. The entire class was transferred to the Carlisle and Barrow area in 1962, remaining there until withdrawn between the end of 1967 and September 1968.

A somewhat chequered career befell another of the Type 2s, the English Electric 1,100 hp 'Baby' Deltic. Nos. D5900—9 had a smaller version of the engines fitted in the Class 55 Deltics and spent their entire working lives in the Kings Cross area. Appearing in the early summer of 1959, they played an important role in handling the newly-dieselised suburban services. However, while they proved reliable in day-to-day conditions, they were beset by major engine troubles and all had been taken out of traffic by June 1963. They were put into store and then, a year later, they began to reappear, with modified engines, and lasted a few more years until withdrawn between October 1968 and March 1971.

Two similar classes were built by North British with 1,000/1,100 hp engines—one with electric transmission and one, as one might guess, for the Western Region, with hydraulic transmission. The diesel-electrics, Nos. D6100–57, were delivered in 1959/60 and the first 38 were temporarily allocated to the Kings Cross and Great Eastern areas

Left: **Warship-shape, Bristol fashion! North British-built No. D834** *Pathfinder* **looks quite shipshape in green livery compared to its immediate successor D835** *Pegasus* **in decidedly tatty maroon livery at Bath Road diesel depot in June 1967.**/*D. L. Percival*

Below: **Nineteen of the first batch of Swindon-built class 42 Warships were fitted with Dual AWS and some spent their latter lives working over the ex-SR lines from Exeter to Salisbury and on to Waterloo. No. D818** *Glory* **prepares to return west from Waterloo with the 9.00 Waterloo–Exeter St. Davids on Saturday August 6, 1966 while in the background an up Portsmouth fast arrives and rebuilt West Country Pacific No. 34098** *Templecombe* **waits to depart with a boat train for Southampton Docks.**/*D. L. Percival*

until the summer of 1960, when they were sent to join the later examples in Scotland. In June 1963, No. D6123's NBL/MAN engine was replaced by a 1,350 hp Paxman engine, and another 19 members of the class were similarly modified between October 1965 and December 1967. No less than 30 of the unmodified locomotives had been withdrawn by the end of 1967, and the remainder were condemned in August 1968; the 20 modified locomotives were withdrawn between May 1969 and the end of 1971.

When the diesel-hydraulics, Nos. D6300–57, were delivered in 1959–62, nearly all were sent to Plymouth, but examples were later to be found at Newton Abbot and Bristol Bath Road. In the mid-1960s, Old Oak Common depot received an allocation, and members of the class then worked empty stock trains into and out of Paddington, as well as London area freight and parcels trains. The class was withdrawn over the same period as their diesel-electric sisters.

Although at the time of writing there are still ten locomotives in service, the Beyer-

Peacock (Hymek) 1,700 hp diesel-hydraulics have steadily decreased in numbers since the first two were withdrawn in September 1971 and the remainder are earmarked for early withdrawal. The class of 101 locomotives, Nos. D7000–7100, was built during 1961–64 and took over secondary passenger and express duties on the Western Region's Bristol, South Wales and, later, Worcester/Hereford lines.

One of the first main-line diesels to appear was the British Thomson-Houston Bo–Bo Type 1 with an 800 hp Paxman engine. Nos. D8200–43 were delivered between November 1957 and February 1961 and were mainly confined to the Eastern Region's GE section, although the first ten were originally allocated to the London Midland Region Devons Road depot and a few examples were stationed at Finsbury Park. Apart from the latter, the entire class was allocated to Stratford by 1968, when withdrawal commenced, and the last 23 were withdrawn there in March 1971.

Stratford depot was also the home of the North British 800 hp Type 1s, Nos. D8400–9. These were delivered between May and September 1958 and were employed on London area freight and parcels duties until they were withdrawn from service ten years later.

A departure from the earlier Type 1s was seen when the Clayton design appeared in September 1962. This had two 450 hp engines, each housed in a low 'bonnet' either side of a spacious central cab, giving good visibility in both directions. By April 1965, Nos. D8500–8616 were in service on the Scottish, North Eastern and Eastern Regions, but those on the Eastern Region joined the majority of the class in the Scottish Region about a year later. In 1967/8, Nos. D8500–35 were transferred to the London Midland Region, at Carlisle, and some of these had the distinction of being withdrawn from service on more than one occasion! All but three of them (which were returned to Scotland) were withdrawn towards the end of 1968, but a number were subsequently reinstated by the Scottish Region. With-

Although introduced in the same year, similar in appearance and employing the same power unit, the Class 22 B-Bs—of which No. D6338 is seen (*left*) in store at Bristol Bath Road Diesel Depot in June 1967—differed from Class 29 in having hydraulic instead of electric transmission. Both classes had chequered careers and soon began to disappear. Some of the Class 29s, however, were re-equipped with 1,350 bhp Paxman engines, including No. D6114 seen (*above*) at Dundee Tay Bridge with the 17.50 to Glasgow Buchanan St. on May 10, 1966, and consequently survived a little longer./*D. L. Percival (2)*

Right: Another type to undergo drastic surgery to the engines were the class 23 'Baby Deltics'. Here the first and last of the batch, Nos D5900 and D5909, climb up to meet the main line at Langley Junction with a Palace Gates–Whitemoor train on June 13, 1968.

drawal of the entire class was completed by the end of 1971 and among the last to go were three of those originally condemned by the London Midland Region; No. D8529, in fact, was withdrawn no less than four times—at Carlisle twice in 1968, and at Haymarket in October and December 1971!

Probably the shortest-lived diesel locomotive type of all time was the Swindon-built 650 hp diesel-hydraulic 0–6–0 Type 1. Fifty-six, Nos. D9500–55, were built between August 1964 and October 1965, and were allocated to Bristol (Bath Road), Cardiff (Canton) and Old Oak Common depots. Designed for trip freight working, they featured a cab mounted near the centre of the locomotive, overlooking low 'bonnets' to provide good visibility for shunting movements. Their introduction unfortunately coincided with widespread closure of small freight yards and a decrease in the duties for which they were intended. By the end of 1966, several were in store and 33 of the class were transferred to Hull Dairycoates depot. Withdrawal began on the Western Region a year later, those at Hull went in April 1968, and the class became extinct in April 1969. Many were under four years old when they were withdrawn, and some lasted for less than three years.

So a dozen classes of main-line diesel locomotives have passed into railway history. But the story does not end there. Examples of most of them can still be seen.

British Railways themselves are using a Swindon-built "Warship", a Metrovick Co–Bo, a Baby Deltic and a couple of Clayton Type 1s at Derby Research Centre, as well as three or four BTH Type 1s converted for use as carriage heating units. Another of the Claytons is in use on an industrial line, and nearly all of the Swindon 0–6–0s have found a new career—for which they are eminently suited—on NCB, quarry and other industrial systems. An appeal is being made to save No. D601, which is rusting alongside steam engines in Woodham's yard at Barry, and Swindon-built "Warship" No. 821 *Greyhound* has already been preserved.

And on the subject of preservation, it is perhaps arguable whether any of the types described here are worthy of a tangible place in railway history but, surely, some of them are. The 'preservation era' came too late for some notable classes of steam locomotive—will it also bypass those diesels which were unfortunate enough to be withdrawn while 'steam' was still fresh in the memory?

Right: **The MetroVick Type 2s, of which D5714 here is an example, were neither the most successful nor the most beautiful of machines, but they were nevertheless unique in their unequal Co-Bo wheel arrangement. After an early spell of working in tandem on Midland line express freights, they spent their last years in the Furness area.**

Bottom left: **Unlike some of their sisters, the 56 Swindon-built Paxman Class 14 Type 1 diesel hydraulic 0-6-0s Nos D9500-55 suffered short careers on BR—some lasted less than four years, and none more than six—not because they were inefficient, but because the freight trip-working they were built to perform simply disappeared. A costly mistake on the part of BR, much of their lives was spent in store, as here at Hull Dairycoates depot in May 1967. Almost all were eventually sold for service on industrial lines.**

Below and right: **When the Clayton class 17 Type 1 Bo-Bos first appeared in 1962, they were generally thought to be an improvement on earlier designs, with their lower engine room profile and centrally-placed cab giving good all-round vision. But ten years later, almost all had been withdrawn and cut up—a fate which had all too clearly befallen D8600, the remains of which were photographed at Glasgow Works in April 1973./D. L. Percival (4)**

Southern in the Snow

Above right: **A sudden overnight snowfall such as this, with snow piled high on the conductor rail and around trains stabled overnight at outlying stations, is hardly conducive to punctual running! Rebuilt West Country Pacific No. 34009** *Lyme Regis* **swings across to the Down Local line at Surbiton with the 8.35 Waterloo–Weymouth train on a winters day in 1962, while in the background, a quick-frozen 4-SUB departs for Waterloo on an up stopping service from Hampton Court.**/*Alan Williams*

Below: **Almost every winter, commuters from South of London can be heard to complain of the Southern Region's vulnerability to a few flakes of snow. But to be fair, no system with such close headways and a high incidence of points and crossings as the Southern's— quite apart from its peculiarly vulnerable conductor rail system—can reasonably be expected to escape some delay from adverse weather conditions. In steam days, it was at times like this that travellers on the non-electrified lines looked rather smug! Here, BR Standard Class 4 2-6-0 No. 76066 restarts a Salisbury–Yeovil stopping train away from Semley on December 27, 1962.**/*G. A. Richardson*

Below right: **After a swift 5in snowfall, a Hampshire diesel electric multiple-unit sets out from Netley beneath laden skies on a Salisbury–Portsmouth working on December 8, 1967.**/*J. H. Bird*

Left: **A light dusting of wet snow, followed by a sharp frost, is just the formula for trouble with iced conductor rails. In typical SR winter weather, 4-VEP unit No. 7740 leaves Ifield on a Bognor Regis–Victoria working in February 1970.**/*Colin Gifford*

Right: **The 16.14 Victoria–Brighton stopping train, formed of 2-BIL and 2-HAL units, pulls away from East Croydon in a snowstorm on March 4, 1970.**/*Michael Baker*

Below: **It is January 12, 1963, and West Country Pacific No. 34103** *Calstock* **is in for a long wait here in the up siding at the south end of Oxford Station, because the southbound "Pines Express" which it is booked to work forward to Bournemouth is reported running 2½ hours late. Now** *that* **can't be the Southern's fault!**/*C. P. Walker*

Left: With Merchant Navy Pacific No. 35014 *Nederland Line* **in charge, the 10.30 Waterloo–Weymouth hurries through Holton Heath Station on January 14, 1960.**/*R. A. Panting*

Right: **Before the diesel "tadpoles" took over the service, SR U class 2-6-0 No. 31793 brings a Reading–Redhill train into Betchworth, at the foot of the North Downs near Box Hill, on a snowy day in March 1964.**/*G. D. King*

Below: **Because they have to await so many connections along their route, cross-country trains often suffer severe delays during widespread bad weather. One such casualty on December 8, 1967 was this Cardiff–Portsmouth Inter-City dmu, hurrying through Netley on the last leg of its journey several hours late.**/*J. H. Bird*

Metamorphosis
on the other GCR

E. J. ALYSON

Left: **Double-headed by Maunsell S15 class 4-6-0 No. 837 and Great Central-type Pacific No. 1947** *Eureka,* **a lengthy summer Sunday train hurries along the double-track GCR main line among the trees below Cockrow Hill.**/*Alan Williams*

Below: **LMS Stanier Black 5 4-6-0 No. 4571 rests in the platform at Hardwick Central while beyond, LMS 4-6-0 No. 6100** *Royal Scot,* **SR S15 Class 4-6-0 No. 837 and GCR No. 1947** *Eureka* **are prepared for traffic.**/*Hugh Saunders*

To many people—including myself—miniature railways are something of an oddity—a sort of narrow-gauge line with shrunken replicas of main line locomotives. And, most of all, nearly all miniature railways belie their description, for they are almost always disappointingly short, often with nothing more than a stretch of track, one overworked steam engine and a couple of coaches. And that, to my mind, is not a *railway*.

So it was with a certain degree of scepticism that I first went along to see the then Greywood Central Railway in Burwood Park, Walton-on-Thames, back in 1959. A local newspaper had waxed lyrical about the Railway, and I had determined to see for myself whether its claim to be the largest miniature railway in the country was in any way justified. I have to admit that I was converted at first sight. The then owner of the line, the late Sir John Samuels, showed me a railway which in every way justified the lavish praise bestowed by the newspaper article; Walt Disney, a keen railway enthusiast and for many years an Honorary Vice-President of the GCR, once told me that he had often seen larger miniature lines in the USA, but never one quite so complete as a railway.

Over the next few years, I came to know the GCR very well; in particular helping to complete and work the fully-interlocked 27-lever signalbox at Burhill, which controlled the main line of the GCR, including the stations at Jacksonville and Mount Hoyt, and the locomotive depot at Broad Oak. There were two lengthy tunnels on the line, including one which passed directly beneath Mount Hoyt station, two handsome brick-built viaducts, and a splendid skew flyover spanning the low level approach lines to Jacksonville Station.

Sir John Samuels began to build the line around the grounds of his house, Greywood, shortly after the Second World War, and by the early 1960s the line had grown to a fully-fledged Weekend Railway, complete with a stud of over half a dozen locomotives, a vast selection of passenger and freight rolling stock, engine diagrams and working timetables, full mechanical signalling and a host of other items of equipment. Basically, the line was a continuous single line circuit with passing loops at Jacksonville and Mount Hoyt, a return spur to enable out and back working, and two branches, one leading to the depot and main terminus, Broad Oak, and the other running up through a tunnel alongside the house to the other terminus, sited in the front garden at Greywood North. It was a fine railway, and the small group who ran it were all as keen as mustard; I can remember helping an enthusiastic gang to shovel about a foot of snow off the entire ¾ mile-long line one Christmas in order to run a 'Santa Special'—and this was long before any of the Preserved Railways had thought of it!

Then came the untimely death of Sir John, and the entire future of the Railway was thrown into doubt, for the house and grounds had to be sold. As a group, we found ourselves in the unique position of having a Railway with nowhere to go! In the event, Ian Allan, Chairman of Ian Allan Ltd., came to the rescue, and the metamorphosis began. In an incredible exercise which would have done credit to the Royal Engineers, every salvageable item on the railway was carefully dismantled, cleaned, catalogued and packed. Soon the once-busy yard at Broad Oak was piled high with reclaimed track, the signals were dismantled, and the signal boxes stripped of their fittings, while the locomotives, rolling stock and everything else moveable was greased and prepared for transit and an extended close season.

Within a few weeks only the now-trackless lofty brick viaducts and silent tunnels remained, looking for all the world like memorials to a miniature Beeching. But this particular railway was to rise again.

Over the next few months, we began to clear and level the ground at the new site of the railway, some five miles away on a farm at Cockrow Hill, Lyne, near Chertsey. We acquired two condemned railway containers from BR as Mess and Tool huts, promptly re-christened the railway the 'Great Cockrow

Railway' and set about the construction of a new locomotive, carriage and wagon depot complex. The very first structure on the new line, the turntable giving access to the seven-road engine and carriage sheds, was completed in September 1966. From then on, construction proceeded apace, and the first section of the line was opened in the Autumn of the following year. The continuous circuit form of layout, with a return loop, had served us well at Greywood, and we resolved to build much the same again, although there was now more space, and therefore no need for expensive and time-consuming spirals! As the Civil Engineering Department finished the considerable embankments, cuttings, bridges and culverts, so the Permanent Way gangs followed up with pre-assembled track and ballast, with the Signal and Telegraph people following up in the rear, erecting signals, laying wires and equipping signal-boxes.

By the start of the 1970 Summer Season, the four-track terminus at Hardwick—named after the Lane it serves—was complete, together with a single-track circuit some half a mile in length, with a return loop to allow out-and-back running, and stations with passing loops and signalboxes at Phillips Bridge and Everglades. The growth of traffic during the Summer of 1970 was such that, in the following year, doubling of the main line throughout began. This necessitated the widening of the embankments, cuttings and culverts, but was nevertheless complete by 1972, allowing the intermediate signalbox at Phillips Bridge to be closed, the junction here now being controlled by fully-interlocked multiple-aspect colour light signals worked from an extension to the frame in Everglades signalbox. In the past few years, additional facilities have also been provided at Hardwick, including a new locomotive run-round spur behind the engine shed, enabling the erstwhile spur in the station to be converted into a fourth platform road.

As the line has grown, so too have the problems of maintenance; more and more

Below: **Memories of the Greywood Central: Gresley LNER K5 2-6-0 No. 206 waits to leave the yard at Broad Oak with a train of loco coal.**

Bottom: **Now departed from the GCR, GW 4-6-0 No. 7915** *Mere Hall* **waits for passengers at the Greywood North terminus of the old Greywood Central Railway.**

time has to be spent on keeping the track in first-class condition for main-line running, and in keeping the locomotives, rolling stock and signalling equipment in good working order. And all this is quite apart from the non-railway but equally essential work of hedging, ditching and repairing fences. Nevertheless, further extension of the line around Cockrow Hill to a new terminus is planned, and it is hoped that work on this project will start during the 1974/75 Winter Season.

Meanwhile the locomotive stock of the line continues to grow. Two LMS Stanier Black 5 4-6-0s, an LNER K3 2-6-0 and an 0-6-0T have arrived to join the five engines that came across from the original line—a GCR-type Pacific No 1947 *Eureka*, LMS 4-6-0 No 6100 *Royal Scot*, LNER K5 2-6-0 No 206, LNER D19 4-4-0 No 1239 and SR S15 4-6-0 No 837. Members of the group are variously working on a "Britannia" Pacific, a BR Standard 9F 2-10-0 and an LBSCR Atlantic. In addition to all this steam power, there is an LMS jackshaft-drive 0-6-0 diesel shunter and a four-wheel diesel *Thunderbolt*.

But despite the extensive nature of the line, and its large locomotive stud, perhaps the most remarkable feature of the Railway, as on its predecessor at Greywood, is the comprehensive signalling system. Passengers on GCR trains enjoy as much protection signalling-wise as any on BR; the 19-lever signalbox at Hardwick is fully interlocked, and trains between Hardwick and Everglades Junction signalbox, which controls the main continuous circuit and return loop, are worked on the absolute block system. Everglades Junction signalbox has 28 levers controlling points and crossovers, and both semaphore and colour-light signals; a considerable section of the main line in the Phillips Bridge area is now equipped with fully track-circuited multiple-aspect colour light signals, and several signals in the area can, at the signalman's discretion, be switched to purely automatic operation. As this part of the line is remote from any signalbox or station, lineside telephones are provided at intervals for use in case of emergency or failure.

The present signalling allows trains to run to as little as 90-second headways, and at busy periods it is quite usual for the Everglades signalman to have up to five trains, all moving under his direct control. It does, however, require a high degree of concentration, swift blockwork and agility with the levers to *keep* five on the move!

All the signals on the line are scale models, with both upper and lower quadrant semaphore arms in use; an impressive six-arm gantry has recently been completed at the approach to Hardwick Station, and work is now progressing on signal alterations in connection with the proposed extension round Cockrow Hill. This will be single-track and protected by token working, for which purpose two instruments have already been acquired. Many eminent people in signal engineering have visited the line, including one retired Inspecting Officer (who happily made no adverse recommendations!) but perhaps the greatest compliment to the signalling staff on the line comes from a retired signalman who often comes and sits quietly by one of the signalboxes—not to watch the trains, but to see "a real live signalbox in action".

The new GCR has grown once again into a complete railway; most Sundays in Summer one can stand on the slopes of Cockrow Hill and see perhaps five trains in motion at once, all running at express speeds and fully protected by modern semaphore or colour-light signalling. Happily, the number of passengers carried continues to grow each year, and visiting parties from railway societies throughout the country are once again a common—and welcome—sight. In addition, each year sees more visiting engines, brought to the line by their owners to be put through their paces on what is now perhaps the only steam-operated double track main line in the country. Certainly at times on Summer Sundays it operates at a frequency to rival the Great Eastern 'jazz' service in its heyday.

Towards
the Tunnel?

MICHAEL RIGBY

The preliminary works for the Channel Tunnel that, as these words are being written, have begun on both sides of the English Channel are visible proof that, at last, the long and chequered history of attempts to forge a permanent physical link between England and France has taken a new and perhaps hopeful turn.

The works are part of the second phase of the Channel Tunnel project, a phase that began in November 1973 with the signing of a treaty and commercial agreements between Britain and France. A special Act authorises expenditure of some £30 million on design studies and preliminary works on the British and French coasts and the driving of 2km of service tunnel from both sides. This work is scheduled to be complete by mid-1975, when a final decision on whether or not to go ahead, and agreement on the terms under which finance will be raised, must be reached.

All being well, the main Channel Tunnel Bill in the British Parliament and parallel legislation in France will give powers to construct a 49.26-km rail tunnel between Cheriton near Folkestone and Sangatte near Calais, comprising two single-line running tunnels flanking a service tunnel, terminal areas in Britain and France and links with the rail and road networks of both countries. Barring further physical and political setbacks, the dream of a high-speed, high-capacity rail link between Britain and the Continent should finally come true by 1980.

Innumerable words have been written on the engineering feasibility and political expediency of a Channel Tunnel since 1802–3 when, during the truce in the Anglo-French war of 1793–1814, a French mining engineer named Albert Mathieu showed his plan for a Cap Gris Nez to Folkestone tunnel, including an artificial island created on the Varne Bank, and Tessier de Mottray proposed a submerged cast-iron tunnel. Both ideas were way ahead of their time and in the event the resumption of war put paid to them. Incidentally, it is interesting that at the outset just as in recent years an immersed tube vied for favour with one bored through the chalk bed of the Straits of Dover.

From the 1830s onwards few years passed without new projects for a Channel tunnel or alternatively a bridge. Some were of great merit and based on sound engineering principles, others wildly fanciful or impractical. All make fascinating reading and those who seek a good account of them cannot do better than to study A. S. Travis's *Channel Tunnel*, published in 1967.

In the latter part of last century the great British champion of the tunnel was Sir Edward Watkin for whom it was to be the *pièce de résistance* of a grand design for a through trunk rail route between Manchester and Paris which would, on the English side, be formed of sections of line owned or projected by the companies which he chaired. Watkin's plans were largely frustrated in the end by his rivalry with J. S. Forbes of the London Chatham and Dover Railway and the antagonism of military men haunted by the spectre of trainloads of French legions descending on England through the tunnel! But at least Watkin's pertinacity resulted in sections of pilot tunnel being driven on both sides of the Channel, from Shakespeare Cliff and Sangatte, before a halt had to be called.

Recalling perhaps that a son of Brunel had once been concerned with a Channel project, William Collard produced at the end of the 1920s an ambitious plan for a 7ft-gauge electric railway between London and Paris which included twin 23ft-diameter tunnels under the Straits. Collard's scheme was one of a number examined by a committee that reported to the Government in February 1930, its finding being that a tunnel would benefit British economy. When a subsequent motion in the Commons in favour of a tunnel was lost by only seven votes, a promising opportunity passed. This defeat decided the Southern Railway to go ahead with what culminated in 1936 as the Dover–Dunkirk "Night Ferry" service which, save for the period of World War II, has functioned ever since, its now ageing compromise-sized Wagons-Lits stock bringing a daily Continental look to Victoria Station.

World War II made nonsense of the strategic objections that had bedevilled every attempt to promote a fixed Channel link since the 1880s and the now favourable climate of opinion was expressed by Harold Macmillan in the House of Commons in 1955. Leo d'Erlanger, chairman of the British Channel Tunnel Company—an undertaking dating from the 1870s—and Leroy Beaulieu, a director of its French counterpart, took new heart, and gained the support of the Suez Canal Company in financing a revived tunnel scheme. Other influential backing was secured

and in April 1957 the Suez company, supported by the two tunnel companies, was able to announce the setting-up of a study group including British, French and American interests.

Over the next four years the Group spent £750,000 on a marine and geological survey and on economic, traffic, revenue, engineering and other studies. The work even included an examination of the samples of French surveys of the 1870s which, as Mr Travis writes, were found in a disused Paris station.

A working group of British and French officials reported in September 1963 in favour of a tunnel link in preference to a bridge or the continued use and development of existing means of cross-channel transport. A major political step forward was made in February 1964 when the then British Minister of Transport, Ernest Marples, said that the British and French governments had agreed that the construction of a tunnel was technically possible, that it would be a sound investment of resources and that, subject to more discussion of legal and financial problems, they had decided to go ahead with the scheme. Further investigations followed in

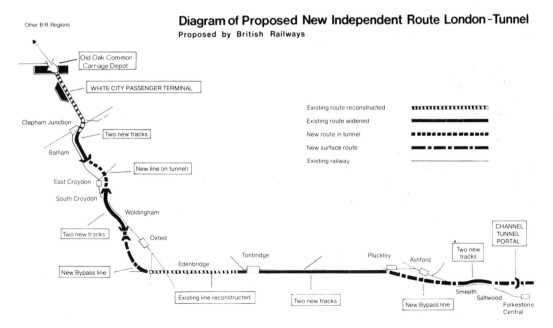

Diagram of Proposed New Independent Route London-Tunnel
Proposed by British Railways

Other B.R. Regions

Old Oak Common Carriage Depot

WHITE CITY PASSENGER TERMINAL

Clapham Junction

Two new tracks

Balham

New line (in tunnel)

East Croydon

South Croydon

Woldingham

Two new tracks

Oxted

New Bypass line

Edenbridge

Existing line reconstructed

Tonbridge

Two new tracks

Pluckley

Ashford

Smeeth

Saltwood

New Bypass line

Two new tracks

CHANNEL TUNNEL PORTAL

Folkestone Central

Existing route reconstructed

Existing route widened

New route in tunnel

New surface route

Existing railway

July 1966. Harold Wilson, the British Prime Minister and Pompidou, the French Prime Minister, reaffirmed their governments' support.

In October 1966 the two governments confirmed the basis on which studies of relevant problems would proceed and stated in particular that the tunnel would be financed by a group of private financial interests which would also manage the construction. On completion, the tunnel would be taken over by an Anglo-French operating organisation.

In March 1971 the British and French Ministers of Transport accepted proposals from a group interested in financing and building the tunnels. The group comprises 22 organisations, including BR and SNCF, banks and finance houses. The 11 members of the British sub-group are founder shareholders of the British Channel Tunnel Co. Ltd. and the 11 of the French sub-group are founder shareholders of La Société Française du Tunnel sous la Manche. Parallel agreements (Agreement No 1) concluded in October 1972 between the governments and members of the group provided for financial, economic and technical studies to be completed by mid-1973 and set a framework for action should the project go forward. Half of the £5 million cost of the studies was to be found by the companies and half raised under Government guarantee.

The 1972 agreements were superseded by Agreement No 2 signed on the same day as that of the Treaty by Mr John Peyton for the United Kingdom and M. Billecocq for France and setting out arrangements for financing and building the tunnel.

The year 1973 saw the publication of both a Green and White Paper, exhaustive reports and studies, including a detailed economic review, a United Kingdom transport cost benefit study, and—indicative of the growing concern for environmental aspects—a 260-page report by economic consultants on the likely economic and social effects of the tunnel on Kent.

It is estimated that at 1973 prices the tunnel will cost £464 million and that final costs, including inflation and interest charges, will total £846 million. The cost will be borne equally by the two countries. The sum of £84 million as risk capital will be repaid by a private company which will build and operate the tunnel. The remainder will come from loans guaranteed by the governments.

Responsible critical comment at the time of the Anglo-French signings in 1973 included that of the journal *New Scientist* whose October 11 1973 issue included a close examination of all aspects of the scheme. It questioned whether the Straits had surprises in store for the tunnellers in view of the fact that trial bores in the Upper Chalk near Shakespeare Cliff showed a 'rotten zone' of weathered chalk persisting downwards for more than 30 metres, a discovery necessitating a late realignment of the tunnel route which in fact saved 2.5 km.

As *New Scientist* stated, the test borings now in progress will show how fast the main tunnels can be driven, how much water may infiltrate, how much ground movement may be expected and how the boring machines perform. The length of the tunnel is not a special problem. Many longer non-transport tunnels (albeit not under-water) exist and the Japanese are driving a slightly longer rail tunnel through the rock below the Straits between Honshu and Hokkaido. The drawback is that an under-water tunnel cannot be driven from more than the two working faces at each end, so that the fast cutting rate of 9.6km/h is proposed to keep down costs.

The test bore engineers will probe the Lower Chalk by drilling holes ahead of the borers. The holes will have valves so that they can be sealed off if a wet zone is struck. Special grouting clays will then be pumped in. Sideways probing from the service tunnel will explore layers which the two main tunnels will traverse.

Cross passages every 250 metres will link the running tunnels with the service tunnel and sufficient rail crossovers will be installed to allow bi-directional working over any section during maintenance work or failure. The running tunnels will probably be about 7 metres in diameter but the exact diameter depends on the outcome of present studies of the size of road vehicles likely to be conveyed through the tunnel which will in turn affect the size of the wagons to carry them.

The tunnel will reach its greatest depth at 110 metres below sea level. The ruling gradient will be 1 in 100 and the minimum radius curves will be 4,200 metres.

The White Paper describes the proposed signalling system for the tunnel as one which 'will be required capable of maintaining a space interval between trains adequate for safety. It should incorporate some form of safeguard to prevent the passing of signals at danger' and be 'capable of development to provide control of the train's speed at any point using the most advanced techniques available'. A speech communication link to the controlling signalbox will be provided at all stop signals. A carrier wave telephone system or its equivalent will be needed as a link between trains and the tunnel control centre.

Stringent safety regulations for the tunnel will necessitate fitting fire doors or curtains with a resistance time of at least 30 mins to vehicle-ferry wagons.

The service tunnel, giving access to the main running tunnels via adits at 250m intervals, will have its own quite separate transport system to enable emergency services to reach any part of the tunnel quickly even if the main running tunnels were to be blocked. Continuous walkways are to be provided on each side of the track throughout the length of both main running tunnels. Emergency lighting will be available at all times in both the service and running tunnels, and to further guarantee supplies, two separate sources will be used, each able to provide 'a sufficient intensity for personnel to move about in safety'. All fixed equipment in the tunnel will, as far as possible, 'be of fire-resistant materials and of a nature that, when exposed to fire or electrical discharge, does not give off toxic fumes or dense smoke'.

Nevertheless, should a fire occur, the ventilation equipment will be capable of maintaining a smoke-free area into which passengers could be moved pending evacuation from the tunnel. One of the basic operating requirements specified in the White Paper is that 'in the event of a train becoming immobilised in the tunnel for any reason, it must be possible to ensure that any other trains in the tunnel can be brought out without delay and that all passengers, including those from the stranded train, can reach the open air within a period not exceeding 90 minutes'.

The tunnel is an exciting prospect for British Railways, for which it offers the possibility of long hauls and much increased passenger and freight through movement, including, it is hoped, important passenger traffic captured from air services.

The draft basic passenger service is for hourly departures from London to Paris and to Brussels, with some trains starting from Manchester or Birmingham and continuing from Brussels to Amsterdam or Cologne. The proposed initial timing of 3 hours 40 minutes London to Paris and 3 hours 25 minutes London to Brussels compares very favourably with air timings involving city–airport transfers. Overnight sleeping car services are planned from London to French, Spanish, Italian, Swiss, Austrian, German and Dutch destinations. In addition, charter trains may run where an economic proposition; they would operate overnight, with couchette stock. Consultants estimate that about $8\frac{1}{2}$ million passengers will use the tunnel in the first year after the tunnel opens and 12 million by 1990, compared with the 1972 figure of 4 million—apart from those in their own cars—using the Dover, Folkestone and Newhaven boat services.

Motorail services from the Midlands, South Wales and the North to Southern France, Italy, Switzerland and Southern Germany are also planned. In addition there will be drive-on/drive-off shuttle services between Cheriton and Fréthun, the British and French tunnel terminals, of car-and

Southern Region Oxted line diesel-electric units Nos 1301 and 1308 growl away from Clapham Junction on the 15.55 Victoria–Uckfield on August 15, 1973. The proposed new independent high-speed link from White City to the Tunnel would follow the Oxted Line formation between South Croydon and Woldingham and, if a surface route is adopted, here at Clapham Junction would cut through the ground immediately behind the train to gain access to the West London lines which diverge from the Victoria Lines beneath the overbridge in the background./*Brian Morrison*

lorry-carrying trains. Loops at the terminals will enable such trains to run at up to 4-min intervals. Cars will be conveyed in either double-deck wagons or in single-deck wagons which can also carry coaches and caravans. Lorries and trailers will be conveyed separately on single-deck wagons. An area at Stanford nearby would be reserved for stabling and maintaining ferry wagon stock.

Despite assurances from the Government that the proposed Cheriton terminal will be designed to blend with the environment as much as possible, a strong body of conservationist opinion favours an 'all-rail' tunnel solution that would dispense with a terminal near the tunnel portals.

Freight services will include fast freightliner-type block trains to carry containers from London and provincial centres to many Continental destinations. Trainloads of bulk commodities and other trainload traffic would also operate. Such trains would enable, say, fruit and vegetables to be carried swiftly and directly from the growing areas in southern Europe to British markets.

Of the present rail routes from London to the short-sea ports only the straight section from Tonbridge onwards is suitable for really high-speed running. Other sections could be upgraded only at enormous cost in building cut-offs and new tunnels. In addition, no route leading to an existing London terminus suitable for handling the traffic is free from severe curvature and other operating restrictions in the London area. Accordingly, British Rail plans a brand new high-speed route 80 miles long from the coast to London, to be electrified, like the tunnel line, at 25kV. Between Saltwood and Tonbridge it will run first on the north side and then on the south side of the existing well laid-out main line, a cut-off between Smeeth and Pluckley avoiding Ashford. Inwards from Tonbridge, where another deviation may be built to avoid the station and junction, the route will absorb the existing Redhill line as far as Edenbridge. There, a new line will diverge, curving north-westwards, west of Oxted, and threading the

North Downs by a new tunnel, probably west of the existing Oxted tunnel on the Croydon–Oxted–Uckfield line.

The Oxted line will be gained near Woldingham and the Channel Tunnel line will run alongside it. The Oxted line will be singled in part, to give room for the newcomer on the existing formation in a district where the railway clings to the eastern slopes of the Caterham Valley. Even so, some tricky work will no doubt face the engineers as the Oxted line, though its ruling gradient of 1 in 100 will not be a serious handicap, has sweeping curves which may need realignment.

Inwards from South Croydon, junction of the Oxted and main Brighton lines, the density of the built-up area and the complexity of the BR network will preclude a continuance of the Channel Tunnel line on the surface. Between South and East Croydon stations the new line will therefore enter a tunnel extending to near Balham, on a straighter course than the existing line through East Croydon, Thornton Heath and Streatham Common. Thence to Clapham Junction there will be no great difficulty in finding room for the new line alongside the existing line.

Originally, three possible London terminals were considered: Victoria, the present Continental 'gateway'; and two new sites, one at White City, reached by the West London Line, the other at Surrey Docks, reached from the London Bridge–Croydon line at New Cross. Victoria may possibly be served by some Channel Tunnel trains but it is already used almost to capacity and reconstruction would be exceedingly costly. A terminal at Surrey Docks was at one time supported by the Greater London Council in the context of dockland redevelopment but appears to have receded from favour.

The intention is therefore to build the main Channel Tunnel terminal at the White City, 'to a high architectural standard', on land owned by BR. Not only could a White City Station be tailor-made for the traffic, but it would also have excellent connections

with the London Midland main line, enabling trains from the Midlands and North to the Continent to serve it. Moreover, it has satisfactory underground railway and road links which could be improved as necessary and is close to suitable stabling facilities at Old Oak Common Depot.

The West London makes an awkward connection with the former LBSC side of Clapham Junction. The present reverse curve through the station, flanked by platforms 16 and 17, will need to be straightened but slow running will still be necessary on to the West London. An alternative solution is to build a direct new line in tunnel from a point between Wandsworth Common and Clapham Junction under the Thames to the West London at Chelsea.

Incidentally, the proposed use of the Oxted line brings the wheel full circle in a sense as the Caterham gap was the outlet first chosen for the South Eastern Railway, which, however, Parliament compelled to go via Redhill, sharing a route through the North Downs with the Brighton line until friction with the LBSCR and the opening of the shorter LCDR route forced the South Eastern to build its costly New Cross to Tonbridge cut-off via Sevenoaks, opened in 1868.

On the French side, Channel Tunnel trains for Paris or Brussels will first use existing routes which are electrified only in part, but the SNCF and SNCB propose to build a new high-speed line on the 'Europolitain' concept from Paris to Brussels with a spur from near Lille to the tunnel, enabling the London–Paris time to be cut to some $2\frac{1}{2}$ hours by using stock capable of operating at up to, say, 185 mph. BR has favoured using an electric version of its APT but such tilting-body stock, though suitable in many other respects, would have no great advantage in operating over new high-speed routes with their easy curves.

Rolling stock on through services operating north of London would necessarily have to conform to the British structure gauge and in this connection BR has in mind a possible development of its new Mk III stock.

Battling towards Blaenau

Top right: **Clinging to the hillside on the climb up to Dduallt,** *Merddin Emrys* **nears the present inland terminus of the Festiniog with the 14.00 from Portmadoc on August 19, 1971.**/*G. F. Gillham*

Middle right: **"What are they up to today?" seems to be the question on the minds of the crew of** *Merddin Emrys* **as they round the corner past Boston Lodge Works on the last leg of their journey down to Portmadoc with the 14.20 from Dduallt on May 27, 1972.**/*J. Scrace*

Below: **Festiniog Railway Fairlie 0-4-4-0T No. 10** *Merddin Emrys* **coasts downhill between Campbell's Platform and Tan-y-bwlch with a train for Portmadoc on Whit Monday, 1968, shortly after the section up from Tan-y-bwlch to Dduallt had been re-opened.**/*A. G. Cattle*

Bottom right: **Even nearer its destination, Festiniog 0-4-0ST** *Linda* **trundles off the Cob and into Portmadoc Harbour Station with the 15.11 from Dduallt on August 30, 1972.**/*G. D. King*

Left: **With flanges squealing, one of the Festiniog's more recent acquisitions, the Alco** *Mountaineer* **storms round Tylers Curve on August 24, 1972 with the 12.30 Portmadoc–Dduallt train.**/*J. Scrace*

Top right: **Rattling across the lane into Penrhyndeudraeth comes 0-4-0ST** *Blanche* **with the 10.20 Portmadoc-Dduallt on May 30, 1969.**

Before and after pictures that happily reverse the general trend on most British railways. The desolate scene *Bottom right* (**there** *are* **some tracks beneath the undergrowth!**) **is Minffordd FR station in August 1953, while** *Middle right* **is the same view 18 years later on June 24, 1971, with** *Merddin Emrys* **restarting a train for Portmadoc, while another bound for Dduallt waits in the loop. A tribute indeed to the management and volunteers alike of the Festiniog Railway!**/*M. E. Ware, G. S. Cocks*

Below: *Mountaineer* **was equipped for oil burning in the Winter of 1971/72, but until then sported a splendidly un-British spark arrester. Here she curves off the Cob past Boston Lodge Works with the 10.15 Portmadoc–Dduallt on July 29, 1971.**/*P. H. Groom*

Left: **There are occasional failures even on the best of railways; Gardner diesel** *Upnor Castle* **helps** *Mountaineer* **into Tan-y-bwlch after the latter had failed with injector trouble on a Portmadoc–Dduallt working on July 20, 1971.**/*P. H. Groom*

Right: **Even older than the oldest locomotives on the Festiniog is this little bridge across the road to Tan-y-bwlch. Just 111 years after it was built in 1854, 0-4-0ST** *Linda* **rumbles overhead with a train down to Portmadoc on August 2, 1965.**/*M. Dunnett*

Below left: **Limited clearances seem not to worry the crew of** *Merddin Emrys* **as she blasts through the cutting on the last few yards of the climb into Tan-y-bwlch station with a Dduallt train on September 1, 1969.**/*G. J. Warrilow.*

Below: **Restarting her heavy nine-coach train round the curve out of Tan-y-bwlch comes 0-4-0ST** *Blanche* **with the 14.15 Portmadoc–Dduallt on July 23, 1969.**/*G. F. Gillham*

Left: **Setting back on to its train ready for the return trip downhill to Portmadoc comes Fairlie 0-4-4-0T** *Merddin Emrys.* **The bridge and embankment under construction in the background will form part of the spiral at the beginning of the new deviation line around the CEGB lake at Tan-y-grisiau to Blaenau Festiniog.**/*J. R. Barton*

Right: **It is a continuous climb practically all the way from Boston Lodge to Dduallt, so 0-4-0ST** *Blanche* **pauses to quench her thirst at the water tower at Tan-y-bwlch before continuing the climb with a heavy afternoon train in July 1968.**/*Alan Williams*

Below right: **Original engine, new stock. To cope with the rapid increase in the number of passengers over the past decade, the FR have either re-furbished or built new several handsome bogie coaches. Here original Fairlie** *Merddin Emrys* **prepares to depart from Dduallt for Portmadoc with some of the newer stock on September 7, 1972.**/*G. D. King*

Below: **Less than a decade ago Dduallt was a deserted halt, over-run with the lush vegetation of the area after a quarter of a century of disuse. But now, every day throughout the summer season it is a scene of much activity as trains come and go, as well as providing the "base camp" for work on the new extension.** *Mountaineer* **is ready to depart back to Portmadoc on July 30, 1971.**/*I. G. Holt*

The Lonely Line

DEREK CROSS

Below: **Having joined the West Highland main line
from the Caledonian Oban branch, North
British Class 29 Bo-Bo No. D6107 restarts a
Glasgow-bound train away from Crianlarich
on April 15, 1968.**/*Derek Cross*

The Fort, the Covenanters Canon and the Black Wood of Rannoch. Sounds like the makings of a Witches Sabbath, but in fact just all part of the West Highland story.

The Fort was Fort William, built by one of King Billy's minions in 1690 to keep the Highlanders of Lochaber in order. Needless to say, it didn't, and the West Highland Railway put it to much better use as an engine shed when that lovely but lonely line was completed from Glasgow to the shores of Loch Linnhe in 1893. The Covenanters Canon likewise never fired a shot in anger, for it is a rock high above the western side of Loch Lomond at the entrance to Glen Falloch. Even today it remains unseen from the road, for this was the main aim of the Covenanters—they had to remain out of sight of any road traversed by the troops of the Establishment. The West Highland Railway shows less respect and skirts about its base; from the cab of a modern diesel growling up towards Crianlarich it is a remarkable sight—something that the last Ice Age forgot. What then of the Black Wood of Rannoch? What a name for what a place! It is the westernmost remnant of the old Caledonian Forest, slowly dying now after surviving the great fires that burnt from Kingussie to Bridge of Orchy. Botanists may argue about it, photographers rave about it and romantics write sonnets to it, but the West Highland Railway simply passed right through it. There is something different about the Scots 'native' pine, with its cedar-like growth, when compared with the Scots Fir, which the Forestry Commission have obligingly planted nearby as a comparison. In fact, it is not the Black Wood that stirs the imagination, but the sinister name of Rannoch that is coupled to it; a wood, be it black or any other colour, is a small thing in comparison with that great upland bog of Rannoch Moor, the refuse heap of all the glacial debris of West Central Scotland. It is truly a haunted place and even on a fine summer morning it is frighteningly lonely. There is mile after mile of moss and heather bog, with the odd great granite boulder

dumped here and there to mark the time when the climate warmed and the glaciers got tired. On a clear day, the mountains loom all about: the sinister cone of Schichallion, to the east, the elegant peak of Ben Dorain in the south, and to the west and north the ranges of Appin and Lochaber.

In the early days of railways the Liverpool and Manchester line had to cross Chat Moss, described by Robert Stephenson at the time as a "bottomless father of a bog". Compared with Rannoch Moor, Chat Moss was little more than an ill cleaned ditch; furthermore, Chat Moss is in the centre of the major industrial area of Northern England and is thus easily accessible, whereas Rannoch is in one of the remotest parts of western Scotland, and is not only virtually unknown but was much feared by those whose livelihood was gained near its edges. Even today, the roads avoid it, skirting westwards down Glencoe or up the Garry, far to the east. General Wade looked at it and wisely decided to avoid it, although there was a battle fought there in the '45 for some totally obscure reason. Yet the West Highland Railway decided to cut clean across it, floating the foundations for its tracks on a bed of brushwood and sheepskins. It was an act of faith without parallel in the history of British railway building, and it nearly killed the engineer, surveyors and promoters, for they set out, with all the rectitude of Victorian times, to walk across this fearsome place in spats, top-hats and tail coats at the end of January in the unkind winter of 1889! They survived more by luck than good guidance, and their brainchild is with us yet. There can be few contrasts in railway or other forms of social engineering as shattering as that between the teeming, constricted streets of Glasgow and the vast emptiness of Rannoch Moor in a distance of only 80 miles. It is an interesting point to consider whether a shepherd of the moor would feel less at home in Glasgow than a Glaswegian sent out on the moor. One thing is certain—I know who would have the better chance of survival!

Why, you might ask, build a railway out in

BRCW Class 27 No. 5367 waits to depart from Glasgow (Queen Street) with the 10.05 Glasgow–Mallaig on September 5, 1972, the day of the trip described./*Derek Cross*

these wild places at all—especially as late as the 1890s? Why indeed! By that time the railway mania was over and people no longer assumed that steel, once laid on sleepers, turned to gold—far too many had their fingers burned in the process. The reasons for the being of the West Highland are varied. For a start, there was the usual one in railway history, never admitted, that you built a railway in order to stop somebody else doing so. At varying times the Caledonian and, even more unlikely, the Glasgow & South Western, cast acquisitive eyes at Lochaber, and there was always the Highland lurking just across the Grampians. The most important declared reason for the building of the West Highland was the improvement of communications for the farmers and the fishermen of the area, so that they could get their products to the lucrative markets of the south. Tourists also figured in the West Highland calculations, but to a lesser degree than miscellaneous livestock or fish. There

were also two other reasons—the first was the determination of the inhabitants of Lochaber to have their own railway, and the second, more subtle, was the opening up of the vast uninhabited tracts of country north of Loch Lomond. Now this concept was unusual in Britain, where railways were historically built to link existing centres of population and industry. However, it was far from unknown in British Colonies abroad and so in some ways the West Highland's concept could be seen as a plan to bring people back to places where the sheep had taken over during the notorious Highland Clearances.

In none of its intentions either declared or unofficial was the West Highland wholly successful. Despite the construction of the West Highland, the Caledonian built a line up from Connel Ferry to Ballachulish, on the doorstep of Lochaber, the fishing fleet stuck to the East Coast ports, and although Fort William got its railway, the inhabitants were few and passenger traffic never really showed a profit. Lastly, the displaced persons from the Highland Clearances, having tasted the dubious delights of big city life preferred these to the solitude of the West Highlands. Yet despite Beeching and the economists, the line survives, thanks to aluminium and timber, and the determination of the local people to retain their rail link with the south that they fought for so hard and so long.

To many people whose interest in railways was more of an aesthetic experience than a means of transport, all enthusiasm died with the end of steam, the newer forms of traction being dull and soulless things which were noisy, smelly and predictable. For a long time I suppose I felt the same way, but a recent trip in the cab of the diesel heading the 10.05 Glasgow (Queen Street)—Fort William changed my mind, for although I had travelled the West Highland by train many times in all weathers, this was something completely new. For the first time I saw the line as it must have been in the mind of Charles Foreman, its great engineer, when he first set out to survey it. The old Highland proverb "If you'd seen these roads before they were made, you'd bless the name of General Wade" unfolded before me for four glorious hours, on a day of late summer sunshine with the threat of rain to come later adding a piquancy to the experience.

Apart from the first two dozen miles to Craigendoran the West Highland is no main line of fast trains and great engineering works; this is a line that has to use every feature of the landscape to its advantage as it twists and claws its way between the great hills of north-west Scotland, round the head of deep lochs of salt or fresh water or across the wastes of the dreaded Moor of Rannoch. Just as Foreman and his engineers had to use every trick they knew to build the line, so the driver and his mate on the trip to Fort William have to deploy a lot of experience to run the train to time. Modern power means modern schedules, and modern schedules on a run as continuously curved and steeply graded as the West Highland give little time for the enginemen to sit back and admire the view. If the diesel epoch means that the romance of railways is dead, then it is taking a considerable time a'dying on the West Highland. The privileged passenger in the cab of a diesel hauling a train to the north-west would surely have to have a heart of lead if he was not thrilled by the first few hundred yards of single line from Craigendoran Junction as the coast is left behind and the single line pushes through the rock cuttings and the trees into the unknown, with only a glimpse of the now-electrified Craigendoran Pier below to remind him of the urban sprawl he has left behind. Or again of the climb far above Loch Long, when time and again the line looks to be heading into a buttress of solid rock and only takes avoiding action at the last moment. Or of the conical peak of Ben Dorain, dead ahead as the train claws its way over the summit at the County March between Perthshire and Argyll north of Bridge of Orchy, with the rails dipping down out of sight to the Horseshoe Bend ahead, and above all, the Moor of Rannoch. Such glimpses are what the 'Romance of Railways' means; the fact that a steam engine might have made more noise or more smoke is as relevant as a good sauce to a fillet of sole. On a winter night on Rannoch Moor, the challenge is man against the elements, and whether his tool is steam, diesel or even a wheelbarrow does not matter, so long as the goods reach their destination.

The contrast starts at once. The newly-renovated platforms of Glasgow's Queen Street station—clean, well lit and concrete—are confronted by the dark arch of Queen Street tunnel, for over a hundred years the terror of eastbound drivers in steam days and even now a challenge to more modern forms of motive power, for it is still damp and odiferous. Once over the top of the climb to the old Cowlairs Station and its winding house, the West Highland line bears away to the north and within a few miles joins the electrified suburban lines to Dumbarton and Helensburgh at Westerton Junction. Then for some 14 miles the railway runs along the flat north bank of the Clyde Estuary, with the great river glimpsed occasionally between the decaying shipyards and oil terminals. To parody Tennyson, "On either side the railway lie...long lines of council houses...God knows why!" The 10.05 does its best to keep out of the way of the frequent, bustling electrics, gets a passing blast from the guardian geese of a large whisky warehouse and blending plant on its eastern side and stops briefly at Dumbarton Central. Soon after restarting, the line crosses the River Leven, draining down from Loch Lomond, once renowned for salmon and, thanks to some spirited cleaning, likely to be so again soon. Then a last look at the dark satanic mills and forges of the Victorian era before suddenly the train is running on a low embankment at the very edge of the tidal waters—so near in fact that on a winter night with a south-west gale the sea blows across the tracks at high tide.

'Frontier Town' is a term well known to all addicts of westerns and if ever there was a 'frontier junction' Craigendoran Junction, some 25 miles from Queen Street, must surely be it. Behind lies the great urban and industrial sprawl of the Central Lowlands while ahead lie the great hills of the unknown far North West. Even the name is more Gaelic than Glesca in its nuances. This is urban sprawl in reverse, for whereas in most of the realm towns spread further and further into the country, at Craigendoran the great hills thrust a defiant foot into the urban door. We were stopped at signals on the sea wall just short of Craigendoran Junction for a few minutes, giving me time to take in the contrast of the urban scene we had just left, the waters of the Clyde to the south-west and the overhead wires of the electrified suburban line still hugging the coast on its way to Helensburgh, with the tip of Craigendoran Pier just showing round the next corner. There was a typical brick-built signal box

directly ahead, every gaunt line proclaiming its North British origins and to the east of this a line curving into a wooded cutting. A line of mystery, it might have been going anywhere or nowhere—and in a sense the West Highland did both! The driver turned to the Motive Power Inspector accompanying me, saying "Dougie, it's that bluidy Oban late again— it's been late every day this week". A couple of minutes later the much abused train appeared out of the trees, the crew handed their tablet for the single line section to the signalman and with a far from contrite fanfare on its horn departed on its way for what many would call civilisation. Seconds later we were away; the signalman handed us the tablet for the single line section on to Garelochhead and we were on the West Highland proper, our diesel snarling where once steam engines roared. Up through the banks of rhododendrons and steep rock cuttings with now only tantalising glimpses of the widening firth below. A brief stop at Helensburgh (Upper) station and on again against the rising grades with all the power that oil and modern technology could provide. Only 30 miles from Glasgow we were already in the Highlands!

The climb to the first summit at 564ft sets the scene for much of the line south of Crianlarich. There are rock cuttings, incessant curves and, through the trees, tantalising glimpses of the waters of the Gareloch below and the mountains of Argyll rising on the far side. These glimpses are fewer now than ten years ago, for the diesel locomotive does not have the vegetation burning tendencies of its steam predecessors—no doubt a gain to the neighbouring farmers, but a loss to passengers wanting to see the passing scenery. Between Helensburgh (Upper) and Glen Douglas there used to be, in addition to Garelochhead, three small wayside halts with the sonorous names of Rhu, Shandon and, most unlikely of all, Whistlefield. Like many pipe dreams they have gone now, for they served towns that never were! In 1893 when the line was opened the great rush to suburbia was in its infancy and the promotors hoped, with some justification, that the salubrious airs and great vistas of the hillsides above the Gareloch would attract businessmen from Glasgow to build there, provided there was a convenient station. The stations were duly built, but alas the businessmen's 'commodious residences' did not follow. One of the ironies of optimism is that the old station house at Shandon has been converted into a most attractive bungalow, the occupant having to go to Helensburgh for his supplies by car as there is now no other way! Garelochhead remains, and on my journey its role as a crossing place was fulfilled, for in the up platform was a lengthy goods train waiting to head south. The next crossing point, at Glen Douglas, also boasted a southbound goods train, for thanks to the new aluminium and paper mills in the Fort William area the West Highland is now carrying more freight traffic than at any time in its history.

From Garelochhead to Glen Douglas the line crosses a saddle in the hills between Gareloch and Loch Long, but the traveller not armed with a map could well be excused for not noticing. Only for a mile is the railway out of sight of a great sea loch and from high on a hillside and among the lineside trees one sea loch looks very much like another. The station at Glen Douglas is closed now but the signal box and sidings remain, the latter surrounded with high barbed wire, for nowadays they are used for 'military purposes'—whatever that may mean. Anything, I suppose, from ration books to radar parts!

Beyond Glen Douglas the railway still twists and turns among the trees high on the hillside, but it is no longer climbing and for the next four miles drops slowly to Arrochar and Tarbet station. The West Highland was never over-endowed with money, so with the two villages only two miles apart, the company decided to build a station half way between them and name it after both! It was not a bad compromise as it happens, but what a difference between the two villages! Arrochar to the west is on the sea at the head

of Loch Long, while Tarbet to the east is on Loch Lomond, a matter of 50 feet higher; the narrow, shallow valley between the two nowhere rises above 100ft. Looking down from the train, one wonders what would happen if a small earthquake opened up this narrow valley. Luckily earthquakes are virtually unknown in Scotland!

Like many of the stations on the West Highland Arrochar and Tarbet is set on a hillside. Just below it is the steeple of what appears to be a church, but despite its outward appearance as a place of worship—stained glass and all—it is now a garage! There must be a lesson in this; could it be that we now all go to heaven in motor-cars? From the present highly dangerous state of the A82 road up Loch Lomondside, this would seem to be more than likely! Certainly it is this road that keeps this novel garage at Tarbet in business.

Still, in the cab of 5367 we had no worries on this score and the run up the west side of Loch Lomond as far as Ardlui was in many ways a repeat of the 15 miles before—curves, rock cuttings, trees and brief glimpses of that famous great sheet of fresh water. The power station at Inveruglas is hard by the line, although the halt built while it was under construction has long been demolished. Ardlui is a crossing station at the head of Loch Lomond. It marks the end of great loch vistas for the next 45 miles, and the start of serious climbing among the great hills of west-central Scotland. The first test of locomotives in these hills, be they steam or diesel, is Glen Falloch bank. It is short but steep and very sharply curved, and was one of the most dreaded of all of the great gradients on the West Highland in the days of steam. It also boasts the first of Charles Foreman's workmanlike viaducts of steel girders on stone piers, built on a graceful curve over the Dubh Eas gorge; from here on to Fort William they are a feature of the line and an enduring tribute to Scottish railway engineering. The summit of the climb up Glen Falloch comes only a matter of half a mile from Crianlarich Station; there could be few more apt places,

Oban, for when the West Highland was opened the enmity between that Company, as a protégé of the North British, and the Caledonian was submerged at least for long enough to allow them to agree to build a connecting line from Crianlarich (Upper), on the West Highland, down to Crianlarich Junction on the Caley's Oban line a few hundred yards west of Crianlarich (Lower) station. Prior to Nationalisation in 1947 this spur was seldom used despite protestations of goodwill on the parts of both the LMS and LNER, but now it is Oban's only link with the south. Poor Crianlarich, down there in its inter-montane valley for many centuries, has had an importance thrust upon it by geology and geography it didn't really want and has never been able to live up to; first the old drove roads, then the railways and now the motor car. It has a charming, if rather rain-prone situation, and deserves its peace. Alas, the bellowing of bullocks gave way to the snorting of steam locomotives and now the maniacal moanings of motor-cars.

As we pull away, the spur to Oban tumbles away to the west off the end of the station platform, looking exactly like the afterthought that it was. But the West Highland line strides on, across those remains of the Callander and Oban still in use over a few hundred yards for conveying logs from the forests of Strath Fillan to the great new pulp mill at Corpach, and then across the River Fillan on yet another of Charles Foreman's elegant and functional stone and steel viaducts and thus to the hills. "I to the hills will lift mine eyes" wrote the Psalmist; it is a stirring phrase, but the effort involved by the Psalmist in lifting his eyes to the hills was

for not only is Crianlarich the half way point between Glasgow and Fort William, it also marks the end of the deciduous trees which have clustered about the line most of the way from Dumbarton. From here on the few trees that can be seen are all conifers, the struggling survivors of the native pine seen on the eastern skyline at the head of Glen Falloch being every bit as much the start of the Highlands as any mythical 'Highland' line.

What a strange place is Crianlarich, for while it is and always has been a key point on the route from the Central Lowlands to the north and west of Scotland, the River Fillan that it straddles flows to the east, to enter the North Sea at Perth! In happier times there was a line that came in from the east through Strath Fillan—the old Caledonian's line from Stirling to Calander and Oban. But a landslide in Glenogle a little over a decade ago put paid to that, although luckily without catastrophic results to the train service to

nothing by comparison with the effort needed by the West Highland Railway to get through them.

For the West Highland the effort starts here. Once Strath Fillan is crossed, the line hugs the southern flanks of Ben Challum and climbs for seven miles at grades mostly as steep as 1 in 60 to County March summit, beyond Tyndrum Upper Station. Below the train to the south west the old Caledonian line to Oban twists on the other side of the valley beneath hills quite as gaunt and bleak as those facing us to the north. Between the two there is a scene of geological devastation equal to that seen anywhere in Scotland, for it was here that several of the great glaciers of the last Ice Age got tired, melted away and decanted their loads of boulders, clay and other detritus scraped from the great hills to the north. It must have been a spectacular thaw! A short stop at Tyndrum gives time to notice the surrounding belt of trees,

a feature common to many of the more exposed stations, specially planted by the West Highland Company for shelter. Then we are away again, out onto the slopes of the great hills, which are becoming noticeably barer, for this is the high, wild country of tremendous gales. Then suddenly, as the locomotive growls up the ferocious grade, there comes a vista surely without parallel on any British railway. As the line tops the 1024 ft summit at the County March and dips down into the valley of the River Orchy, the whole scene to the north is dominated by the nearly perfect cone of Ben Dorain. It is a unique experience, especially as the railway can be seen ahead, but some hundreds of feet below snaking northward like twin silver threads around Dorain's flank. We get there via the 'Horseshoe Bend', probably the most famous of all the engineering features on the West Highland. It is a perfect horseshoe in shape and possibly the only justified case for the use of the term on any railway. It also contains two more of Foreman's sturdy truss girder viaducts. Dwarfed by the great hills whose bases it skirts, the railway looks a fragile and tiny thing—and in times of great blizzards it is—but for 80 years it has linked Lochaber with the industrial South and the rest of the World.

Beyond the Horseshoe Bend comes Bridge of Orchy, the last station with any claim to contact with the relative fleshpots of the west coast and Oban. Again, this is a typical West Highland structure, with an island platform surrounded by trees. Beyond, the railway turns to the east, closely hugging the hillsides, while the road which has been our near companion all the way from Arrochar turns away to the west and the Pass of Glencoe. For the next four miles the railway climbs gently (by West Highland standards!) with the lakes and rivers of the Tulla Valley opening up below. Burn after burn tumbles off the flanks of the high hills to the east while ahead looms the Black Wood of Rannoch. A strange place this, because, since we passed the head of Loch Lomond, trees, other than

those windswept Scots firs especially planted about the remote West Highland stations, have become increasingly scarce. Seen from the cab of a northbound train, the West Highland cuts straight through this living fossil. The fact that on our trip we were obliged to crawl for some few hundred yards where orange-coated men were busy relaying the track in our path only served to heighten the contrast between the living railway to Fort William and this dying remnant of the once great Caledonian forest. Beyond, trees and houses are few and far between; the odd few houses for railwaymen cluster about the remote stations, while increasingly the Forestry Commission are scattering their drab woods of spruce about the moor with what would appear to be catastrophic results.

For the next 20 miles it is steel rails against peat, clay and water; the offspring of the Industrial Revolution versus the remnants of a climatic upheaval. On a summer afternoon the railway wins hands down; on a fierce winter night the balance might be rather more even, with nature holding the trump cards! It could not be otherwise, for the

Moor of Rannoch is a haunted place; not for nothing was the early morning goods on the West Highland known as the 'Ghost'. Driving a train out across these wastes on a winter night with only the marsh lights for company must have been a very strange experience. Fort William men usually worked this train and not surprisingly they can tell many strange tales about it, for even on a warm September afternoon there is nothing about on the moor. It is a part of Britain that nobody wants to know—and who will blame them! General Wade made noises about building a road across these marshes but funked it, and the electricity board erected a few pylons but then took fright and slunk off down Loch Rannoch less than half way across. The West Highland Railway Company beat it, although one wonders if they would have even tried had not the Caledonian been making nasty noises down by Loch Leven. Nobody who has seen the panorama of Rannoch Moor from the front of a train as the last remnants of woodland drop behind can fail to appreciate the utter desolation of the place. It is gaunt, grey and very, very cold, even on a summer afternoon. It is every municipal park ever created rolled into one vast, sterile featureless mass.

Some two miles beyond the Black Wood there used to be a station, built purely for crossing trains in the high noon of the old West Highland. It was named Gorton after a nearby shepherd's cottage; the cottage still remains but the station has gone and only the most perseverent observer could find traces of its existence now, for even in these high desolate parts nature is quick to take over what man has abandoned. From here on the line is out on the bleakest part of the moor and drivers are confronted by a very strange effect, for although the track looks quite level in fact it undulates constantly. Hence I could not understand at first why our driver would suddenly open his throttle, making the powerful diesel engine behind us snarl into life when it looked for all the world as if we were going down hill! There is nothing out among these peat bogs to judge the gradient against—you just have to rely on local knowledge—and strangers frequently make mistakes; there have been cases of trains in the hands of unwary drivers nearly stalling on what looks to be a down grade!

For 20 odd miles the West Highland line twists and undulates across this terrible bog and it comes as a surprise to see any sign of man's hand on it at all. There is a feeling notice way out beyond the ruins of Gorton proclaiming 'Soldiers Trenches'—and there in the blow grass to the west of the line are marks of what could have been trenches, but could equally well have been drainage ditches. Quite why anyone would want to fight over Rannoch Moor is a mystery to me!

Left: **Menacing cloud envelops the mountains beyond as BRCW Class 27 No. 5349 tops Tyndrum Summit with the 13.00 Mallaig-Edinburgh, including through sleepers to Kings Cross, on April 28, 1971.** */J. H. Cooper-Smith*

Right: **Dwarfed by the mountain slopes, BRCW Class 26/1 No 5311 drops down from Tyndrum Upper to Crianlarich with the 7.25 Mallaig-Glasgow on April 28 1971./** *J. H. Cooper-Smith*

Far more startling, however, than the remains of some rather soggy trenches is the first glimpse of Rannoch Station. Coming up from the south the line curves through a short cutting and suddenly there it is—a station, a few trees, a cluster of houses and a white painted hotel right out in the middle of the moor. There is even a road that leads away by Kinloch Rannoch to Pitlochry and Perth and there were actually people waiting for the train. Rannoch Station can be truly described as an oasis—though in a very different climate from that associated with such sanctuaries! Just as an oasis in a desert is a waterhole in hundreds of miles of dry sand, so Rannoch Station might be described as a small dry hummock in a sea of peat and water.

The start northwards from Rannoch has to be seen to be appreciated; the line runs onto yet another stone and steel truss bridge, the longest on the West Highland, although it crosses nothing but a small stream and a large amount of bog, before curving to the east with the gradient steepening and the diesel engine snarling its defiance. Next, it curves back again to head north past the dreaded Rock of Cruach and into a cutting through solid granite protected on both sides by 'snow fences' made from old sleepers and rails. At the far end of this cutting is what looks like a tunnel through relatively level ground; but this is no tunnel in the ordinary meaning of the word—it is the only snowshed on British Rail, built after the line had been in use for some years, and bitter experience had shown that it was up around the Rock of Cruach that the snow demons had their playground and winter after winter covered the moor with feet of snow and filled in every cutting on the line. To stop this nonsense, the deepest part of the Cruach cutting was roofed over and the rest protected by snow fences on either side of the line.

Once out of the snow shed, there are more miles of moor and stream on to the next oasis in the peat at Corrour, this time with no other link with civilisation apart from the railway. Sure, there are some tracks fit only for the Land Rovers that serve the Forestry Commission and give access to the fabled Loch Ossian but mainly the railway station at Corrour is there for operating convenience. Just a few yards beyond this remote outpost of the telegraph and contact with civilisation lies the summit of the West Highland line, 1,347ft above sea level. A small thing compared with the railways of the Andes, or even some of those in the more mountainous parts of Europe, but for the last 12 miles the line has run at a height of over 1,000ft. Yet still the great moist moor of Rannoch lies about the line and the traveller might be excused for wondering if this featureless bog will never end. A mile beyond Corrour Summit it does just this, and in the manner of its ending provides one of the most dramatic contrasts on this line of so many fascinating contrasts. Beyond the summit, the line wanders about the peats and mosses of the moor for a few hundred yards, then curves suddenly to the east, hugging close to the bottom of a vast outcrop of rock and there, right ahead and some hundreds of feet below, is a great fresh water loch—and one moreover which at last drains to the north, for not only are we over the summit, we have also crossed the final watershed; Loch Treig below drains into Loch Linnhie, at the head of which lies Fort William.

For the next five miles the line drops on an even gradient of 1 in 67 along a man-made shelf cut between the loch and the towering flanks of Stob Coire Sgriodain, which at times loom above the line with claustrophobic menace. Nearer and nearer to the surface of the water the train descends until, as the north end of Loch Treig is reached, the line passes through a short tunnel, only a few feet above the water level, treats us to a fleeting glimpse of a dam and plunges into the wooded valley of the River Treig. Neither the tunnel nor the dam were there when the line was opened in 1893; the building of the dam to supply water for the British Aluminium Company plant at Fort William entailed the building of the tunnel as well, for the level of the loch was raised to such an extent that the old railway formation was submerged. As we passed on that September day, a long, dry spell of weather had so lowered the water level of Loch Treig that the original formation was clearly visible—a mute reminder that in the West Highlands the climate still holds all the cards!

From Corrour Summit to Fort William it is downhill all the way, and one can sense a feeling of relaxation on the part of the engine crew once the wastes of Rannoch Moor are left behind. With the diesel engine idling now, the dominant noise in the cab was the strident hiss of the brakes as they were repeatedly applied to keep down the speed round the frequent bends and over the bridge of the River Spean on the sharply curved approach to Tulloch station. The last three stations on the way to Fort William differ from the remainder on the West Highland in having a separate platform for each line—all those to the south have a single island platform between the two running lines. Both the Bridges—Roy and Spean—have no great claims to architectural fame, but Tulloch is the most attractive of the whole journey. Not only is its setting picturesque and peaceful after the bleak miles that have gone before, but the station buildings on the up platform are superb, with a deep, elegant shingled roof that would do credit to many parts of Switzerland. Perhaps such luxuries were justified here, for although it is only ten miles from Corrour and the bleakness of the moor, it is over 700ft lower. Truly is the West Highland a line of contrasts! One might be pardoned for thinking, down here in the Valley of the Spean, that these contrasts were now past, but the railway to Lochaber has one more scenic shot left in its locker—and in some ways it is the most dramatic of all, the Monessie Gorge.

Two miles beyond Tulloch, the valley of the Spean, which has until now been wide and well cultivated, suddenly narrows, forcing the road to Newtonmore, the railway and the river together into a narrow gorge of tumbling waterfalls and wierdly carved rock formations. At one point this mile-long gorge

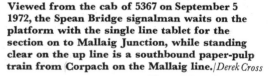

Viewed from the cab of 5367 on September 5 1972, the Spean Bridge signalman waits on the platform with the single line tablet for the section on to Mallaig Junction, while standing clear on the up line is a southbound paper-pulp train from Corpach on the Mallaig line./*Derek Cross*

is so narrow that the railway is built on a stone embankment vertically above the river. Just as suddenly the valley widens again and fields replace the rocks and river, with the little station of Roy Bridge ahead. Between this station and that at Spean Bridge, the river is never far away; but it is tame now, compared with the foaming torrent of Monessie, and shortly before Spean Bridge it is crossed for the last time as the line continues its gentle descent along the northern flanks of Ben Nevis—once described with more than a grain of truth as 'that muckle great flat-topped hill'. It may be Scotland's highest mountain, but it is far from being its most dramatic; as the train pulls away

Above: **Freight traffic on the West Highland has been growing in recent years. Here, BRCW Class 27 No. 5371 rattles past a lonely moorland cottage above Bridge of Orchy with a Fort William–Cadder Yard freight on April 28, 1971.**/*J. H. Cooper-Smith*

But Fort William is our goal and to the 'Fort' we must go, even though the last ten miles must surely be one of the dullest sections of all Scotland's Highland railways. In a strange way this parallels the first dozen miles out of Glasgow, with the grey and crumbling council houses of Clydebank replaced by the serried ranks of the monotonous green conifers of the Forestry Commission. Why have councils and commissions no sense of soul? Thank heaven for the vision of the Lairds of Lochaber and the skills of Charles Foreman nearly 80 years ago, for had it been left to councils and commissions the West Highland Railway would have festered on the footpaths of Fort William or decayed among the dustbins of Dumbarton! Coming down the flanks of Ben Nevis the engine crew prepare for the end of their day's work, the engines idle and the hiss of brake applications comes less frequent as the grades level out on the outskirts of Fort William. No West Highland town can have outskirts quite as depressing as those on the eastern side of Fort William—everything is in a mess. BAC's factory sprawls between the railway and the bottom of Ben Nevis like a dish of spilt jam, while on the other side of the line, garages, motels and scattered attempts at industry are strewn about the banks of the River Lochy with a careless and chaotic abandon.

Then the West Highland plays its last card and gives us yet another dramatic contrast. To the north of the line there is a small signal box bearing the inscription 'Mallaig Junction', and beyond there is an extensive complex of sidings which the stranger could be forgiven for assuming was the main line to Fort William. But it isn't; it is part of the Mallaig Extension, the West Highland's last gasp as an independent company. If the teeming multitudes of Inverness didn't want to know of them, perhaps then the fishing villages of Morar might; but this is another story!

Coming in from Spean Bridge the tablet is exchanged at Mallaig Junction and the train coasts under a road bridge and is

from Spean Bridge and it comes into view for the first time, one sighs for the perfect cone of Ben Dorain or the sinister bulk of Ben More. Spean Bridge for a time had the dubious distinction of being the only junction on the West Highland north of Crianlarich, for it was here that the Invergarry and Fort Augustus railway bore away to the north-east to dream and doze its somnolent way to the west end of Loch Ness, the nearly still-born remnant of the West Highlands vision of getting to Inverness rather than Fort William. Alas Fort Augustus was to remain a place of monks and monsters and has known no railways for many a year.

suddenly in old Fort William. Gone are the factories and motels and, as so often on the West Highland, water lies ahead, this time, that great arm of the sea, Loch Linnhie. Then there are the remains of King Billy's fort, now fuming with expectant diesels, and the signal box controlling the level crossing to the shore, built as a sop to the ruffled feelings of the population who in their anxiety to get a railway at all donated the foreshore to the embryo company. Once the railway came, however, they regretted their generosity and wanted to have their cake and eat it—to have their station and their seaweed-strewn shore as well. In fact, they have got the worst of both worlds; no shore, and a very inadequate station into the bar-gain. Still, inadequate though the station may be, it has its charm, for few other stations can be as near the shore as that at Fort William; step out of the train to the south and you are on the platform, step out to the north and you have to swim!

The West Highland was always a line of contrasts, and what greater contrast could there be than concrete and water? The concrete of Queen Street station in Glasgow is as much a part of the West Highland as the water of Fort William. Houses are around them both, but the bleak moor of Rannoch lies between; it is not only the desolate summit of the line, it is its supreme challenge, and even on a summer day it is a very haunted place.

Below: **One of the regular block train workings seen on the northern part of the West Highland are the Crianlarich–Corpach log trains, one of which is seen here curving past the neat little station at Tyndrum Upper behind Class 27 No. 5355 on the first leg of its journey on April 5, 1971.**/*Derek Cross*

Last Train on the 'Riverside'

ALAN YOUNG

Shortly before electric services on the North Tyneside lines gave way to diesel multiple-units, a single articulated two-car set forms the midday Saturday train from Newcastle to Monkseaton via the Riverside loop at Carville on February 11, 1967. The additional negative rail laid between the running rails on the up line in the foreground was intended to improve the path of the return current./K. Johnson

On Friday, June 20, 1973, without ceremony, the last passenger trains travelled the tortuous $6\frac{1}{2}$ miles of the Eastern Region's Riverside loop between Newcastle and Tynemouth. The five remaining stations on the loop—St Peters, Walker, Carville, Point Pleasant, and Willington Quay—and the branch did not formally close to passenger traffic until June 23, since there was no advertised Saturday or Sunday service. So passed away a line which Dr Beeching had recommended for closure in 1963, but which nevertheless struggled on for another ten years, serving hundreds of Tyneside shipyard employees.

The Riverside was a line fascinating for its anomalies—its blatantly indirect route, its skeletal timetable, and its fully-staffed stations in the Age of the Pay Train, to name but a few. Perhaps its greatest distinction was

that, together with the North Tyneside loop via Wallsend and the Newcastle—South Shields branch, it lost its electric trains at the very time that suburban electrification was being considered for several other British lines.

Authorised on July 13, 1871, the Riverside branch was not opened to regular passenger services until May 1, 1879, the delay being due to constructional difficulties. Engineering works on the line included short tunnels near Byker and Walker, a viaduct over the Wallsend Burn, lengthy cuttings and impressive retaining walls. Stations were provided at St Peters, St Anthonys, Low Walker (renamed Walker on May 13, 1889), and Willington Quay.

By the early years of the present century, the North Eastern Railway was becoming concerned at the decline in passenger receipts on the Riverside branch, and indeed on the whole North Tyneside network. This decline was attributed to competition from the newly-introduced electric street tramcars, so to attract passengers back to the railways, the NER began an experimental electric service on the Riverside branch between Carville and Percy Main on September 27, 1903, and the following year a regular electric service was introduced over the entire branch.

The original electric trains to operate on the branch were of a clerestory-roof type, but these were largely replaced between 1920 and 1922 by elliptical-roofed cars following a disastrous fire at Walker Gate depot in 1918 in which much stock was damaged. The Metro-Cammell trains which operated on all the North Tyneside electric lines, including the Riverside loop, until electric working was abandoned in 1967, were introduced between 1937 and 1939; during their 30 years of service these trains wore no less than four different liveries.

Economies in the operation of the Riverside branch were exercised after the Second World War. The frequency of the passenger trains was reduced, and two of the seven branch stations were closed to passengers—Byker, on April 5, 1954, and St Anthonys, on September 12, 1960. Further economies were to follow in 1967 with the substitution of diesel for electric traction on the North Tyneside line. This change of motive power met with some local opposition, but British Rail pointed out that the change was essential since the electric trains were life-expired. The acquisition of new electric stock was considered to be unjustifiable as the existing electric services had been incurring heavy financial losses for several years.

This attitude towards the suburban services as a whole is interesting when compared with that expressed by the newly-formed Newcastle Passenger Traffic Executive, which now, only a few years later, proposes to re-electrify most of the Tyneside lines as part of a rapid transport system. The Riverside branch, however, is not included in the proposals.

The withdrawal of passenger services on the Riverside branch was first proposed in March 1963 in the *Reshaping of British Railways* report, but a reprieve was granted in the following year pending the construction of a new major road link between Hadrian Road, Wallsend and Bewicke Road, Willington Quay. After reviewing the transport requirements of Tyneside in 1971, the Tyneside PTE decided not to provide financial support for the Riverside line under the terms of the Transport Act of 1968, and in mid-1972, following the completion of the new road link, the closure of the line was once more recommended. On April 17, 1973, official consent was given to the closure of the Riverside branch to passenger traffic on a date not earlier than July 23, 1973, by which time replacement 'bus licenses would have been obtained. It was appreciated that 'a moderate amount of hardship' would be caused to 'a small number of passengers' owing to increased journey time and road congestion, especially to users of St Peters and Walker stations; however, the retention of the service was considered unjustified, since its total annual costs were approximately £100,000 and its earnings only £15,000, and the deficit of £85,000 would have to be met by grants.

It was calculated that within one year of closure there would be a cost saving of £21,000. Interestingly, while economies in the operation of lines have resulted in the singling of tracks, at closure the Riverside branch retained double track throughout its length.

Route

Some of the peculiarities of this line must be mentioned, starting with its route. A glance at the map will show how strikingly indirect the Riverside route was when compared with the alternative line between Manors and Percy Main. A journey between these two stations via Wallsend was fully two miles shorter, and up to eleven minutes faster, than the detour via Carville. In plan the Byker to Carville section described a distorted semicircle, while the remainder ran almost parallel to the Wallsend line for two miles, and for much of this distance the two routes were within sight of one another. On foot it was possible to reach Carville station from Wallsend station in under three minutes, and Willington Quay station was almost as close to Howdon-on-Tyne.

The circuitous nature of the western section of the route was readily apparent to the passenger who took a seat in the front coach of a latter-day diesel multiple-unit to observe the line ahead, particularly dramatic curves

being experienced through Byker station and tunnel, and immediately southeast of the former St Anthonys station where a 10mph speed restriction was enforced. The tortuous route can be explained by the line's function —it was built to serve rapidly growing communities along the north bank of the lower River Tyne which had been bypassed by the Wallsend line. As far as possible the Riverside line followed the curves of the Tyne, although its tracks were adjacent to the river only between St Peters and St Anthonys.

Timetables

The timetable history of the Riverside line is quite remarkable. In August 1887 the Newcastle-Tynemouth passenger service via Riverside operated in both directions on weekdays at approximately two-hourly intervals, while by April 1910 an hourly service operated daily. Bradshaw's July 1938 Railway Guide shows the hourly service supplemented by a variety of extra trains on weekday mornings, in the late afternoon rush hour on Mondays to Fridays, and at lunchtime on Saturdays. The character which the Riverside timetable was to assume in the 1950s and 1960s was emerging, as shipyard commuter traffic began to overshadow ordinary daytime and evening traffic, and the regular all-day services were phased out. By the winter

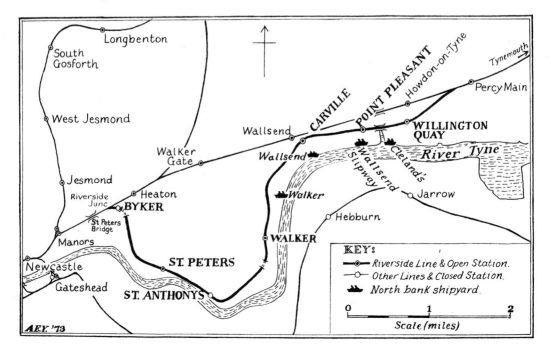

of 1954–55, the Riverside timetable had been drastically simplified to three weekday rush hour workings each way, and two Saturdays-only workings outwards to Tynemouth, one of them advertised to begin its journey at St Peters; only one train operated in the reverse direction. The timetable effective from June 13, 1955 provided a much more extensive and highly complex weekday service. Outwards from Newcastle five trains ran on Mondays to Fridays, but only one on Saturdays. Journeys also commenced for three trains at St Peters, and for one at Point Pleasant. In the up direction, four Monday to Friday trains, one Monday to Thursday train, one Friday train, and one Saturday train arrived in Newcastle directly from the Riverside branch. One of these began its journey at Point Pleasant and two began at Willington Quay, while three further trains in the up direction terminated short of Newcastle at St Peters. Simplification of the timetable followed, and by the summer of 1958 there were only 11 Riverside train columns in the timetable as against 19 in the summer of 1955. The down 12.05 Saturday working from St Peters had been modified so as to depart from Newcastle at 12.00, and this particular working continued until the withdrawal of the advertised Saturday service in October 1970.

It was in the winter of 1961–62 that the Riverside timetable reached new heights of complexity. The Tuesdays and Thursdays working to West Monkseaton from Newcastle via Riverside operated on the evenings in which late shifts were worked at the Tyneside shipyards, but did not appear in public timetables after this date. A series of simplifications followed in subsequent timetables, and on October 5, 1970, the service achieved the final austerity of 06.58 and 16.24 down workings from Newcastle, and 06.20 and 07.45 up workings from Newcastle via Backworth, with another train starting its advertised journey at 16.40 from Willington Quay. An unadvertised train also operated as required on Tuesdays, Wednesdays and Thursdays only for shipyard overtime workers.

This train ran as empty stock from Newcastle at 18.19, arrived at St Peters at 18.26, and began its advertised journey from St Peters at 18.32, calling at all stations to West Monkseaton before returning empty to Gosforth car sheds.

Stations

Anyone who has studied British Rail's Eastern Region timetable in recent years will have noticed that the practically ubiquitous 'No staff in attendance' symbols were always absent from the Riverside timetable, since the Riverside stations were officially fully staffed. However, a visit to the stations at any time but Monday to Friday rush hours would definitely not produce this impression! The booking halls in the sprawling brick bungalows at Walker and Carville would be found empty, and the decaying edifice at Willington Quay could be dismissed as abandoned, while the 'Tickets' signs on diminutive cabins on the down platforms at St Peters and Point Pleasant stations might be entirely overlooked by the daytime visitor. Several minutes before trains arrived in the mornings and late afternoons, a railway official would arrive at these unpretentious buildings, issue tickets from them, collect tickets from passengers alighting from the trains, close and padlock the booking office, and then disappear. Technically, every passenger was attended by station staff.

Being in use for so few hours of the day, the Riverside stations in the later years required few facilities for passenger comfort. At closure, Walker was the station most lavishly provided with buildings. The down platform possessed a booking hall and station house, and a smart brick shelter stood on the up platform, while a functioning signal box of typical NER design stood at the south end of the down platform. In common with many stations in the Newcastle Division, Walker and the other Riverside stations were equipped with very tall vandal-proof electric lamps. Erected in 1969 and 1970, these lamps replaced the less pretentious swansneck electric lamps, which now survive on the branch only at the long-abandoned Byker

121

station. Good lighting was essential on the Riverside branch, since for several weeks in midwinter the stations had no train service in daylight hours. Signposting at Walker consisted of a hand-painted name board in North Eastern Region orange on each platform, and one representative of the previously numerous small cream LNER nameplates, affixed to the wall of the booking hall; the remainder vanished with the old lamp standards. Hand-painted nameboards were used at all of the Riverside stations— neither the orange vitreous enamel metal signs which were erected at all the Backworth/Wallsend line stations, nor the modern black and white 'Corporate Identity' boards ever appeared on this half-forgotten branch.

At closure the down side of Carville station possessed a booking hall of similar style to that at Walker, and a tall brick-built NER signal box. To the last, a conservatory of well-tended pot plants could be admired by eastbound passengers at Carville. The up platform on the other hand was devoid of buildings. At Willington Quay the only building surviving to closure was the decayed brick booking office on the up platform. St Peters and Point Pleasant stations possessed only two buildings each at closure—a ticket booth on the down platform, and a small lock-up on the Newcastle-bound platform. A wooden shelter at Point Pleasant station which leant towards the track at an alarming 10 deg from the vertical was demolished several years ago. Its removal meant no protection against the weather for Point Pleasant passengers, but at St Peters in inclement weather the passenger could seek refuge in the subway and be amused by the rich variety of graffiti on the walls. In fine weather he could be entertained by the activities of a large crane operating directly behind the station in a busy scrapyard. A point of especial interest at St Peters was the wall at the back of the down platform which received its coat of white paint in preparation for a visit to the station by HM Queen Elizabeth, the Queen Mother, in 1961, for the launching of a ship; the undecorated up platform was hidden from view by a strategically parked train!

As to the two stations which closed before passenger services were withdrawn from the branch, St Anthonys had been removed without trace by 1963, within three years of closure, but Byker retained both of its platforms and its lamps and nameboard stanchions until the line itself was closed, 19 years after the last passenger train called.

Since the Riverside stations were staffed until closure, data are available on the numbers of passengers booked and tickets collected. A detailed analysis of the available traffic censuses would undoubtedly show a connection between the fortunes of the individual stations and the prosperity of the shipyards they served, but here it will be sufficient simply to draw attention to some interesting trends in passenger use of the Riverside branch.

The passenger booking figures for 1939 show the following ranking of Riverside branch stations: Walker 52,452; Willington Quay 35,145; St Anthonys 22,702; St Peters 18,050; Carville 17,884; and Point Pleasant 15,145. No data are available for Byker station since, for accounting purposes, it was combined with the nearby Heaton station on the Wallsend and Edinburgh lines. By the mid-1950s, Byker station had lost its passenger service, and St Anthonys, which was to close in 1960, had slumped to the bottom of the list. Willington Quay's share of the passenger traffic had fallen markedly between 1936 and 1957, while Carville and Point Pleasant stations had grown in importance.

Passenger Bookings at Riverside Branch Stations

	1957	1972
Carville	39,197	28,639
Point Pleasant	37,217	19,184
Walker	34,611	18,133
Willington Quay	16,718	4,722
St Peters	11,866	1,868
St Anthonys	11,408	—

The last available figures, for the year ending

December 30, 1972, clearly distinguish between Carville, Point Pleasant, and Walker on the one hand, which served the major north bank shipyards, and Willington Quay and St Peters, which were less favourably situated for shipyard traffic. Although Willington Quay was apparently well placed to serve Cleland's Shipyard of the Swan Hunter Group, the yard was equally well served by Point Pleasant station. The Carville bookings total was the greatest for any of the Riverside stations, but its 28,639 bookings shrink almost to insignificance against nearby Wallsend's 1972 total of 397,734. At the bottom of the bookings list, St Peters booked fewer passengers in 1972 than any other staffed station in the Newcastle Division of British Rail's Eastern Region, with the exception of the isolated Chathill for Seahouses station on the Newcastle-Edinburgh main line. By combining the total bookings and tickets collected at each of the Riverside stations the decline in passenger traffic on the branch in recent years can be appreciated. In 1962 the five branch stations handled 341,200 passengers; five years later the number had decreased to 256,367 and in 1972 only 146,654 passengers used the Riverside stations. To put these figures into perspective, taking bookings alone, the four stations on the alternative Manors to Percy Main route (Heaton, Walker Gate, Wallsend, and Howdon-on-Tyne) together generated over 900,000 passengers in 1972. With the publication in December 1972 of the Tyneside Metropolitan Railway Bill, it therefore came as no surprise to learn that the greater part of the Wallsend/Backworth line was to be developed as a Rapid Transit system, and that the Riverside branch was to be excluded from the re-electrified network. It is interesting to note that in July 1973 only a few days separated the giving of the Royal Assent to the Bill, and the withdrawal of passenger services over the Riverside line.

It was perhaps fitting that the Riverside line was not accorded the honour of a special final train for railway enthusiasts. Instead, the enthusiast had to decide which was to be his final train—the 16.24 departure from Newcastle, or the 16.40 from Willington Quay. If he selected the 16.24 he could claim to have travelled on the last working over the entire branch, whereas if he chose the 16.40 he would have been on the last train on Riverside metals. Few enthusiasts were present to pay their last respects to the line owing, no doubt, to the timing of the last trains during weekday working hours.

Although the Riverside line has officially closed to passenger traffic, it is doubtful whether this will mean any significant changes in the physical appearance of the branch in the next few years. The tracks are to be retained both for goods traffic, which will continue to use the Point Pleasant to Percy Main section, and, if necessary, for passenger trains diverted in emergency from the Wallsend line. Carville and Willington Quay stations might again handle passengers as they have done in the past when diversions have been in operation and Wallsend and Howdon-on-Tyne stations temporarily closed. There might, in future, be another opportunity to travel the ugly, yet fascinating Riverside branch, with its views of the tidal reaches of the River Tyne, and the succession of shipyards, scrapyards, gasworks, decayed stations and abandoned sidings which line its route.

Finally, I should thank Mr D. Deighton, Public Relations Assistant at Newcastle station, for allowing me access to passenger traffic censuses, and for providing a wealth of useful information, and Mr G. R. Larkbey for commenting on the script. For further details of the rolling stock used on the Riverside branch I would refer readers to *North Eastern Electrics* by K. Hoole, and to I. S. Carr's informative article, 'End of the Tyneside Electrics', in *Railway World* for August 1967.

Pacifics
Preserved

Above right: **In the mid-60s, before steam was banished from the Southern by the Bournemouth electrification, preserved A2 No. 60532** *Blue Peter* **climbs away from Woking through the trees of St. Johns up to Milepost 31 with an LCGB railtour.**

Below right: **There are two Britannias preserved, No. 70000** *Britannia* **herself on the Severn Valley Railway and No. 70013** *Oliver Cromwell* **here at Bressingham Hall, Diss.**/*Alan N. Price*

Bottom: **Although a single line from Paignton, the GW line to Kingswear was able to accommodate the heaviest GW locomotives on the system, the King class, so it presented no problems when the present owners, the Torbay Steam Railway, brought in the much-travelled A3 No. 4472** *Flying Scotsman* **as an added attraction in 1973. In pouring rain, the famous Gresley Pacific enters Kingswear station with the 11.45 from Paignton on July 20, 1973.**/*R. E. B. Siviter*

Below: **Looking rather out of place in such rural branch line surroundings, Gresley A4 class Pacific No. 60009** *Union of South Africa* **rolls a short two-coach train along the Lochty Private Railway in Fife on June 18, 1972.**/*L. A. Nixon*

There are more Bulleid Pacifics preserved than any other class of 4-6-2—two Merchant Navies, three unrebuilt light Pacifics, and two rebuilt. *Top left* is unrebuilt No. 34023 *Blackmore Vale* at the Longmoor Military Railway in June 1968 before closure of that line obliged the Bulleid Society to move their charge to her present home on the Bluebell Railway. *Blackmore Vale's* heavier sister, Merchant Navy No. 35028 *Clan Line*, looks in fine fettle in June 1972, *Centre left*, after restoration at the South Eastern Steam Centre at Ashford./*P. J. Fowler, J. Harvey*

Bottom left: After several years on static display at Butlin's holiday camp at Ayr, Stanier Coronation Pacific No. 6233 *Duchess of Sutherland* is propelled through Ayr station by diesel shunter No. D3278 on February 25, 1971 on the first stage of the journey to her present home at Bressingham Hall, Diss./*Derek Cross*

Right: With the camera angle emphasising her elegant lines, Stanier Princess Royal Pacific No. 6201 *Princess Elizabeth* waits for the influx of visitors at a Tyseley open day in May 1970./*J. H. Cooper-Smith*

Below: One of the early results of the easing of restrictions on the use of steam engines for specials on BR lines was the appearance of Gresley A4 4-6-2 No. 19 *Bittern* between Bridlington and Filey on this Hull–Scarborough special on April 21, 1973./*J. H. Cooper-Smith*

The Barnstaple and Ilfracombe Railway

N. J. BRODRICK

October 1970 saw the end of an era in the railway history of North Devon, for the Barnstaple-Ilfracombe line of the former LSWR was finally closed, thus severing the last of the five fingers of the 'withered arm' and reducing the passenger services on the remainder of the North Devon Line to the truncated section from Exeter to a railhead at Barnstaple Junction.

Railways first came to this part of the West Country in June 1838, with the authorisation of the 'Taw Vale Railway and Dock Company'. The Company was to construct a new harbour at Fremington, and from it a standard gauge line to Barnstaple Bridge, the site of the present Barnstaple Junction Station, thereby avoiding the awkward and sometimes dangerous passage up the River Taw to the quays at Barnstaple. There then followed schemes to extend the line, to Bideford in the west, and from Barnstaple to the south east along the Taw Valley (The Taw Vale Extension Railway), to meet the Exeter and Crediton line.

However, due to protracted legal wrangling over the gauge and the alleged misapplication of LSWR capital to further standard gauge interests, the line, now to GWR broad gauge, was not opened until August 1, 1854. The Exeter and Crediton had already opened in 1851, so it was immediately possible for trains to run through from Barnstaple to Exeter. The opening of the Bideford extension followed on November 2, 1855, and through trains from Exeter to Bideford at last became a reality over 17 years after the scheme had originally been proposed. At first traffic grew modestly, the trains taking a leisurely 110 min for the journey from Exeter to Barnstaple. By the summer of 1860, the coastal towns served by the railway were beginning to grow in popularity as holiday resorts. To the north, Ilfracombe, the largest holiday centre in the area, was as yet not even the subject of a Railway Bill; its elders began to feel apprehensive about the future of the town, and decided that the time had come for Ilfracombe to have its own rail connections.

The North Devon Line from Crediton to Barnstaple was eventually leased to the LSWR from January 1, 1863, and formally amalgamated with it two years later. Standard gauge rails were added to the broad gauge tracks in 1863 to enable LSWR trains to work over the line.

Meanwhile, the LSWR, observing the growth of the Great Western's tourist traffic in South Devon, decided that it should attempt to develop similar resorts on the North Devon coast. Thus it was partly to satisfy increasing local pressure, and partly with an eye to future traffic, that a Bill was laid before Parliament in 1864 for a line from Barnstaple to Ilfracombe. It was defeated by the Devon and Somerset Railway, which then proceeded to promote an equally unsuccessful Bill. Eventually, the LSWR made a new approach under the auspices of a nominally independent company, The Barnstaple and Ilfracombe Railway. The Bill successfully passed through Parliament and received the Royal Assent on July 4, 1870.

Construction commenced fairly swiftly, but due to the shortages of local labour and the ruggedness of the country through which it was to pass, the $14\frac{3}{4}$ mile line did not open until July 20, 1874. It was built to light railway standards in an attempt to reduce costs and enable major engineering works to be kept to a minimum; the most notable of these works were the curved bridge across the Taw at Barnstaple and the steep gradients where the line crossed the western slopes of Exmoor at Morthoe. Down trains climbed for three miles at 1 in 40 and then descended for two miles at 1 in 36 to the terminus at Ilfracombe, impressively but inconveniently situated on an embankment high above the Town. Because of the lightweight track, only certain types of rolling stock could be used, and this more or less precluded the running of through trains. The famous 'Ilfracombe Goods' engines were built by Beyer Peacock for the opening of the line, and for several years were responsible for all traffic.

In recent years controversy has arisen over the fact that the line was built as a 'Light Railway', over 20 years before the 'Light Railways Act' was passed in 1896! In fact, the 1896 Act was preceded in 1868 by the 'Regulation of Railways Act', Section 5 of which referred to 'Light Railways' and gave the Board of Trade authority to permit any company which had powers to construct and work a Railway to work that railway as a 'light railway'. This meant that it was subject to a maximum speed of 25mph, an axle load not exceeding 8 tons, and any further conditions that the Board of Trade might consider necessary. It was in fact the general conditions imposed by the Board of Trade in 1868 that were subsequently incorporated in the 1896 Act. Thus it was that the Barnstaple to Ilfracombe line became one of the first 'Light Railways' in the country, its opening preceding the more widely known Act by 22 years.

As a Light Railway the years passed peacefully, local traffic increased and the area enjoyed a new prosperity. Tourism developed, but not to the extent that had been hoped when the line was built, and so in an attempt to improve the line, particularly the through services, the LSWR took over complete responsibility for the line, it being formally transferred to the South Western in 1889.

This action was no doubt prompted by the activities of the Great Western, who in 1887 had commenced to run through coaches to Ilfracombe. As soon as it took over in 1889, the LSWR decided that the time had come to make some very necessary improvements. Practically all of its new Ilfracombe Branch was doubled, in three stages, between 1889–91, and the opportunity was taken to upgrade the track and remove any remaining lightweight rails. The signalling of the branch was extensively improved, gate boxes were built at the more important level crossings, and a new Block post was created at Heddon Mill crossing to break the long section from Braunton to Morthoe and Woolacombe. At Ilfracombe the station was extensively rebuilt, additional sidings were laid and a new 50 lever signalbox was built to control the new layout. The section of line between Barnstaple Junction and Town stations, across the River Taw bridge, remained single, controlled by electric token working, as did the short section across the River Yeo swingbridge, between Barnstaple Town and Pottington Box. The locking for the swingbridge span was controlled by a special lever in both boxes, safe working through the section being governed by an electric token, in this case of the non-returnable type.

These works enabled the train service and standard of rolling stock to be improved, the previous weight restrictions being lifted. Passenger traffic increased over the next two decades and by the summer of 1914 full length holiday trains were being run through to Ilfracombe.

The First World War brought little outward change; some employees joined the Services, traffic declined slightly and the train service was reduced, but otherwise the War had little effect. The subsequent Grouping in 1923 also failed to cause any immediate significant changes. The newly-formed Southern Railway did however carry out some improvements to the North Devon lines, to which it gave considerable publicity. As a result, traffic increased on all lines and on July 19, 1926, N15 4-6-0 No 776 *Sir Galagars* appeared with the Ilfracombe portion of the inaugural 'Atlantic Coast Express', and a legend was born. Throughout the 1930s traffic continued to grow, backed by the dynamic marketing policy of the Southern,

although unfortunately all was not well in some parts; at 9.34pm on Sunday, September 29, 1935, a whistle was heard from Braunton road crossing, on the Lynton Line. Three minutes later *Lew* and *Yeo* appeared round the curve from Rolle Quay, and drew the last train on the Lynton and Barnstaple Railway to a stand. But on the Ilfracombe line itself traffic was still increasing, and it was four years later, with the outbreak of the Second World War, before there were any cuts in services; the bright green of the engines gave way to unlined black and tourist traffic declined sharply.

However, the Southern, never a company to look on the black side, was already planning new and improved post-war services. Far away from Devon, at Brighton, developments that were to have the most profound effect on the 'Withered Arm' in the post-war years were taking place. Early in June 1945 the first of a new class of locomotive left Brighton Works and travelled west to Exmouth

Junction shed. A month later, on July 10, No 21C101 *Exeter*, the first of Bulleid's West Country Class Pacifics, was named at Exeter Central Station by the Mayor, Alderman Vincent Thompson. A little later, a similar ceremony was enacted at Barnstaple, when No 21C105 *Barnstaple* was christened, again in the presence of local dignitaries. Thus there dawned upon the west country a new era of locomotive performance, for the new engines soon proved themselves to be masters of the job. On June 20, 1947 the all-Pullman 'Devon Belle' was introduced, the first Pullman train to work through from Waterloo to Ilfracombe and Plymouth, and the new Pacifics had charge of the train from the outset.

With Nationalisation in 1948, the former Southern Railway west of Exeter became a part of the Western Traffic District of the Southern Region. The Ilfracombe line continued to be controlled by the District Office at Exeter, as previously, and its future appeared secure. However, the line had a number of operating disadvantages which were eventually to tell against it as it faced increasing competition from the motor car. The most serious of these problems was the steepness of the gradients. All down trains had to climb the three miles at 1 in 40 to the summit at Morthoe and Woolacombe, 600 feet above sea level, while in the up direction, at the end of the platform at Ilfracombe, trains were faced with a two mile slog at 1 in 36. It was not unusual for heavy summer trains to be double-headed, with a third

Left: **One of the Bulleid West Country class Pacifics fitted experimentally with extra-long smoke deflectors, No. 34006 *Bude* curves away from Barnstaple Town over the River Taw to Barnstaple Junction with a through train to Exeter and Waterloo on August 2, 1950./C. R. L. Coles**

Below: **Ilfracombe in its heyday: it is mid-morning on August 5, 1933, and SR N class 2-6-0 No. 1845 is preparing to move a train of vintage GW stock out of the carriage sidings while alongside a sister engine of the same class waits with a Southern train for Waterloo./F. E. Box**

engine providing assistance in the rear, as they fought their way up the valley. The section up from Ilfracombe to Morthoe also contained the 67 yard long Morthoe tunnel, the atmosphere of which became quite unbearable after a succession of three-engined trains had stormed through! The single-line sections between Barnstaple Junction and Pottington, although quite short, were a considerable operating handicap; smooth working of the sections required some extremely prompt station work at the intervening Barnstaple Town station and a complete understanding between the three signalmen concerned. Finally, the traffic was not uniform throughout the year, being concentrated into a relatively short peak period at the height of summer, with very poor patronage during the long winter months. To cope with the summer traffic, additional facilities, such as Ilfracombe MPD were required, yet they were only fully utilised for a few weeks each year—a very expensive way of dealing with the problem. The peak traffic also demanded the employment of seasonal labour—one cleaner at Ilfracombe was em-

ployed for seven years, during which time he only ever worked for six months in a year; in the winter months he was laid off and had to find alternative work in the town. The problem of the summer peak traffic, particularly on Saturdays, led to the introduction of cheap mid-week fares, to encourage passengers to avoid the busy periods at weekends; the scheme was also popular with local hotels, who made a point of accepting mid-week bookings. But both Ilfracombe and Morthoe stations—the latter in particular—were remote from the towns they served, and this in the motor age was to prove a considerable disadvantage.

Thus through the 1950s the line continued its placid existence; the sidings at Ilfracombe remained full of coaches, though the coaches

were rarely filled with people. On Summer Saturdays everything appeared to indicate that the line was prosperous—crowds of people waited on the platforms, and full length trains still ran through to Ilfracombe from a variety of major industrial towns in the Midlands. Indeed, it seems probable that the Bank Holidays of 1957 and 1958 were among the busiest days in the history of the line. Never before had the resources of the operating department been so heavily taxed, falling back on the might of Bulleid's light Pacifics as they confidently lifted their ten-coach specials up the valley out of Ilfracombe. But this was purely excursion traffic, once-a-year visitors. Though no one seemed to have noticed, most of the regular travellers had gone.

Ilfracombe always laid great emphasis on its rail connections; as late as 1959 the official guide still devoted half a page to extolling the virtues of rail travel, mentioning such things as mid-week fares and the Saturday through services to the Midlands. The guide also explained the Car Tourist Service, which

Below: **The rails have already been stripped from the disused turntable at Ilfracombe Shed as Warship diesel-hydraulic No. 820** *Grenville* **heads up the gradient to Morthoe with the 11.10 Ilfracombe–Paddington on August 10, 1968. Two years later the line itself was closed.**/*M. Edwards*

Right: **With steam to spare, Bulleid West Country 4-6-2 No. 34002** *Salisbury* **bursts back into the sunlight from the short 67 yard-long Morthoe Tunnel as she storms up the two miles of 1 in 36 to Morthoe and Woolacombe with the 7.42 Ilfracombe–Barnstaple one day in May 1963.**/*G. F. Heiron*

enabled the motorist to send his car overnight from London to Barnstaple Junction (only 15 miles from Ilfracombe by road) by covered van, a reduced rate applying for both car and driver. This service has recently been considerably extended under the guise of Motorail, though the nearest railhead is now Exeter.

The last decade has seen the gradual destruction of the former Southern system in the West Country. With the switch to Western Region control in the early 60s, and publication of the Beeching Report, it became obvious that the days of the secondary lines in the West were numbered. Dieselisation was hurriedly (and badly) introduced, and consequently did little to stem rising operating costs. On October 4, 1965 the passenger service between Barnstaple and Torrington was withdrawn, coupled with a warning that it was also proposed to completely close the Ilfracombe line. Some belated attempts at economy were made— the line was singled and reduced to one section all the way from Barnstaple to Ilfracombe, worked on the 'one engine in steam' principle. The signalboxes were closed, Wrafton and Morthoe stations were reduced to unstaffed halts, tickets being issued by the guards. But these economies, although they presumably cut the deficit, did not even approach the heart of the problem; by now there were simply too few passengers to justify the continued existence of the line. Closure was announced for the end of the 1970 summer service, and the local people accepted the fact; it meant little to them anyway, for they all used the buses, which were now more frequent and had the advantage of serving the centre of the towns, not leaving their passengers stranded on the hillside high above their destination.

Thus it was that, as dusk fell on October 3, 1970 the last train, the 19.55 to Exeter St Davids, pulled out of Ilfracombe amid a blaze of flash-bulbs and cheering crowds (why do people *cheer* when their trains are being withdrawn?). At each station and crossing people who had forsaken the railway came back to watch the passing of the last train. At Barnstaple Town, the press and townspeople, determined that the occasion should not pass unnoticed, were out in force. The train then made its way slowly along the riverside, past the site of the earlier Quay station, and ground its way across the bridge over the Taw. With a warning hoot it entered Barnstaple Junction, the single line token was surrendered for the last time, and after 96 years, Ilfracombe was without a railway again. It will be interesting to see if it now suffers the fate its forefathers feared a century ago!

133

'Madame'

CHARLES LONG

The sultry day was drawing to a sticky close. In the subway approach to the Munich *Hauptbahnhof* silent women proffered religious tracts to heedless, late home-going commuters. We went up the escalator to the station concourse. It was twenty-five minutes to nine. We consulted a Train Departure poster. The 20.52 train to Ostend, the 'Tauern Express' due in from Salzburg at 20.32, was shown as leaving from Platform 15.

A solitary *Postwagen* stood against the blocks in an otherwise empty platform-road. But at a quarter to nine the rest of the train appeared, stealthily backing down, presumably shunted from another platform. As it approached, a railwayman jumped down onto the track and stood, quite composed, in the narrow space between the buffers and gangway of the *Postwagen*. The coaches, all 14 of them, smoothly buffered-up and came to a stand. Momentarily, I wondered whether the *Deutsche Bundesbahn* Rulebook had anything to say on the subject of standing in the path of moving vehicles, but this thought was interrupted by my brother, who asked, "What is the number of your seat?" "Coach 82, Seat 60," I replied.

As it happened, coach 82, an ÖBB corridor second, had stopped opposit e where we were waiting. I clambered in and made my way down the corridor. '*Nr. 60 reserviert*,' confirmed the seat reservation plate in the compartment window. I entered. The only other occupant was an elderly lady, dressed in the fashion favoured by the late Queen Mary. She sat in a corner seat very upright. She had a lot of luggage, most of which was spread out on the two seats beside her. (Why she had chosen to face an all-night journey across Europe sitting up in a second-class compartment I do not know. She was plainly able to afford a sleeper—first class at that.) I swung my grip on to the rack above my seat, which was the window corner facing the old lady. "Monsieur, cette place est reservée!" she said sharply. Startled at being thus admonished in French, I replied in English, "Yes, I know, it's mine—I reserved it," and showed her the reservation ticket.

Meanwhile, behind me, another passenger —a young woman—had entered the compartment and was settling herself in the corridor-corner seat unoccupied by the older woman's bags. She was now quietly taking her leave of a man who hovered in the doorway bearing magazines and chocolates. The elderly lady turned her gaze to the newcomer as I lowered the window briefly to make my own farewells to my brother, who had remained on the platform.

Departure time approached. At the far end of the platform, signals winked green. The guard held his baton aloft. The distant hum of the E10 electric locomotive asserted itself above the other station sounds, and the heavy train began to glide along the platform, out of the station, and into the dusk.

I settled back into my seat. The old lady opposite studied me. She spoke.

"Où voyagez-vous, Monsieur!"

"A Londres," I replied.

"C'est un voyage long."

"Oui, Madame."

"Êtes-vous Anglais?"

"Oui."

"Pourquoi avez-vous visité l'Allemagne?"

"Je suis resté—er—avec—er—my brother —mein Bruder."

My long-unpractised school-French collapsed giving way to rather more familiar— though somewhat limited—German.

"Votre frère," she corrected me, "demeure-t-il?"

"Ja—I mean—oui, Madame."

She looked at me severely. She must have realised that the limits of my conversational ability in French had been reached.

"Aujourd'hui," she said, "c'est nécessaire qu'un jeune homme parle français, allemand et anglais!" She ticked them off on her fingers.

"It's certainly useful," I agreed.

Madame turned to look at the younger woman, who sat in her corner reading her magazine. The young woman glanced up as she flicked over a page and their eyes met.

"Où voyagez-vous, Mademoiselle?" challenged Madame.

"Dans cet train, je vais à Ulm." The reply was decisive, the accent impeccable.

"Etes-vous Française?"

"Non, je suis Canadienne."

"Française-Canadienne?"

"Non, Madame, mais je parle français."

While I understood enough to follow the course of their conversation, I began to feel very relieved that my own French was not up to responding to a bombardment of questions similar to those Madame now fired at our fellow-traveller. It was established that the young woman was on holiday—she was staying with friends in various parts of Europe —she had been away from home for three months—she would be returning to Canada in a fortnight's time. But Madame wanted to know more—much more. Was the young woman married? How old was she? Was that her husband who had seen her off at Munich? (It wasn't!) Who was it then?

How long this inquisition might have lasted uninterrupted, I do not know. But the train had meanwhile come to a stand at the station of Augsburg and two German businessmen entered our compartment. While one took the unoccupied seat between the young woman and me, the other established from Madame that, despite the luggage on it, the remaining corner-seat was, in fact, free. He put most of the bags on the rack and sat down. The train started again. Although the presence of the newcomers, each now reading a newspaper, inhibited resumption of the

cross-compartment questionnaire, the young Canadian woman took no chances. I glanced across at her and saw that she seemed to be completely engrossed in an article in her magazine. When she rose to leave as the train approached Ulm, she caught my eye. The ghost of a smile crossed her face.

The German next to me moved along into the vacated corner seat. The time was now about half-past ten. Madame shifted the remaining bags about on the seat next to her. Half-lifting her knees into the space thus created, she settled back into her corner and closed her eyes. One of the Germans also dozed off. I, too, was tired and indicated my agreement when the other shortly suggested that he should turn out the ceiling light. He also drew the curtains to exclude light from the corridor. In darkness we travelled on to Stuttgart.

At half-past eleven—or indeed at any other time of night—the larger railway stations in Germany appear to be as busy as at any time during the day. When we stopped, there were noises of considerable activity outside the train and much to-ing and fro-ing in the corridor. Although both Germans stirred, Madame slept through the disturbance. But not for long, for—as the train got on the move again—the corridor door slid back sharply, the light snapped on, and an official voice said, "Hier sind zwei Plätze frei!"

Madame awoke, blinking at the Ticket Inspector and at the two expensively-suited, perfumed, olive-skinned men who had followed him into the compartment; her displeasure was obvious as, without ceremony, her remaining belongings were heaved on to the rack and it dawned on her that she would not be enjoying exclusive use of two adjoining seats during the night. When the two Middle-Eastern gentlemen had seated themselves the Ticket Inspector withdrew, switching off the light as he did so.

We settled down again in the dark. Suddenly, the man next to me leant forward and addressed his companion in a stage-whisper.

"Eaz al adrashid sharam al darbi."

135

"Ashramid al bin daram."

In her corner, Madame sighed. The conversation continued. After some three minutes, Madame sighed again, only louder. It had no effect. The conspiratorial exchange went on unchecked. After another five minutes Madame tried again. "Messieurs! Messieurs! Je veux dormir!" announced an imperious voice in the darkness. Evidently this did not impress either. For another half-hour or so the conversation continued—to the accompaniment of sighs and tut-tutting from the direction of the corner seat.

Eventually, however, the unintelligible late-night chat show came to an end. For a while there was silence; then, from the corner opposite another sigh as, next to me, the sudden crackle of silver paper proclaimed that my neighbour had produced a bar of chocolate from his pocket. He ate it fastidiously. Sounds in the darkness told us that he broke off each square individually before consum-

ing it, methodically tearing the wrapping as he went. The 'Tauern Express' rumbled on through the night across Germany. At last we all slept.

I was woken by the sounds of general activity at Cologne, just after four o'clock. Madame also was awake. One of the Germans was evidently getting off here, and was collecting his belongings together—quietly, so as not to disturb the three remaining sleepers. As he slid open the door to leave, a blue-overalled figure passed by in the corridor. It was a cleaner, going down the train to freshen-up and restock the toilets. But Madame had spotted that she carried a dustpan and brush. With amazing speed, she shot across the compartment and summoned the cleaner back, indicating her disgust at the torn chocolate wrappings strewn over the floor. The cleaner did not argue. In between the outstretched legs of the sleepers she swept the offending papers into the corridor and collected them in her dustpan. The commotion woke the chocolate eater of the previous night. Madame glared at him.

On we sped to Aachen. There the remaining German and the two Arabs alighted. Madame and I had the compartment to ourselves as far as Liège, where an unsmiling Belgian entered, took one of the corridor seats and buried himself behind a newspaper.

Approaching Brussels, Madame leant forward and smiled.

"Monsieur," she said to me, "voulez-vous m'aider avec mes valises?"

"Certainement, Madame."

It meant three journeys down the corridor.

"Merci beaucoup, Monsieur," she said as we waited by the vestibule door.

"Cet homme dans le compartiment, il est— 'ow you say—Flemish. 'E would not 'elp me." The train stopped. I opened the door and hailed a porter. As I handed out her bags, our recent Flemish travelling-companion brushed past.

Madame turned and offered her hand.

"Bon voyage à Londres, Monsieur." Then she added with feeling, "Tous les jeunes Anglais sont toujours des gentilhommes!"